Quantum Strategy

Winning Strategies of Professional Investment

Warren H. Lau

Published by INPress International, 2023.

QUANTUM STRATEGY

First edition. April 1, 2023.

ISBN: 979-8215543320

Written by Warren H. Lau.

Table of Contents

To My Family

Quantum Strategy

Winning Strategies of Professional Investment

Warren H. Lau

Published by INPress International, 2023.

QUANTUM STRATEGY

First edition. April 1, 2023.

ISBN: 979-8215543320

Written by Warren H. Lau.

Table of Contents

Chapter 14 - Raw Materials Sector and Correlation Studies

To My Family

Quantum Strategy
Correlation Studies of Stocks/ETF Investment

Introduction to Quantum Strategy

"It takes as little as only one second for any news to change the direction of a stock chart."

• Warren H. Lau

In short, Quantum Strategy is a new school of investment strategy grounded in studying the correlations among stock price movements and various statistically measurable factors.

Stocks generally tend to move with a high degree of correlation. An investor can experience how closely two stocks correlate by observing whether one outperforms or underperforms the average investor's return over time. A correlation of 1 occurs when stocks move in sync with each other, while a negative correlation means they move in opposite directions.

When one stock goes up and the other goes down, the two stocks have a perfect negative correlation (-1). The coefficient is negative, which indicates that as the negative correlation between them increases, the stock tied to the other tends to decline. If the correlation between two stocks is 1.0, their prices move in parallel with their average values.

This measure is referred to as the correlation coefficient and is used to assess the degree and direction of correlation between stocks. Many advisers use equity correlation in advanced portfolio calculations, where it ranges from -1.0 to 1.0.

In the case of investments, correlation is a measure that shows the extent to which the prices of two assets relate to their average. To find the correlation between stocks, you must first determine the average value of each stock. Using the Pearson correlation coefficient, we can determine how closely two stocks correlate.

Correlation should be measured over a period of months, years, or even days to understand how frequently two or more stocks move together. No one can predict market performance over a time frame as short or long as this study, but correlation can highlight instances when certain asset classes are out of sync with the stock market.

Investors holding portfolios in low-correlated assets have the opportunity to benefit from lower-risk returns. In practice, investors who aim to maintain portfolio risks and returns that are not overly concentrated may benefit from rebalancing into lower-correlated asset classes.

When building our portfolios, it is best to invest in stocks, bonds, ETFs, and other assets that do not correlate strongly. In addition to correlation, the realignment of asset allocation, investment strategies, and personnel may evolve over time.

For most investors, the traditional mix of stocks and bonds begins where low-correlation investments come into play. A portfolio is not truly diversified if its holdings are strongly correlated, as this means we can predict how other holdings will move based on the movement of a single asset. Low-correlated investments draw from a rich universe of options, both equities and bonds.

For example, between 1926 and 2013, there was no significant correlation between the U.S. stock market and monthly yields on five-year Treasury bills. Bond prices tend to correlate strongly with the stock market, so many investors use bonds to balance their portfolios and manage risk. Over time, stocks tend to earn more than bonds. And while bonds may not correlate directly with the stock market, they play a crucial role in offsetting equity risk.

One of the tools we can use to lessen portfolio risk is to examine the correlation among our assets and equity correlations. One way to determine the equity risk of your portfolio is to analyze your wealth creation based on its equity correlation. Using equity correlations can help you assess the level of risk you are taking and how you might offset that risk.

Share correlation refers to the relationship among stocks and other asset classes such as bonds and real estate. When developing an investment strategy or selecting stocks for your portfolio, the correlation coefficient is a valuable tool.

The bear market that began in March 2000 tested the principle of balancing a portfolio with low-correlated assets. This article suggests that investors can gain better protection against bear markets by using an investment approach focused on low correlation and a balanced portfolio.

Since high trading volumes are known to correlate with large movements in a company's share price, it is expected that the relationship between news and absolute returns would be similar to the relationship we observe between news and transaction volumes. If yield movement is correlated with the portfolio, investors should wait a few periods before adding new investments to reduce the short-term effects of correlation. This study suggests that the correlation between investments and portfolios should be reviewed regularly.

The correlation coefficient is a value that predicts the degree of movement in relation to other stocks. It measures the relationship between two stocks that move in parallel and the strength of that relationship. Portfolio managers use correlation coefficients to diversify portfolios, and traders use them to trade assets based on the positive or negative correlations between those assets.

Share correlation describes the relationship between stocks and their respective price movements. For investors, correlation is useful when trying to explain the movement of an asset or when comparing a security with a benchmark index to highlight the relationship between variables. Comparing an individual stock to an index is one way to use share correlation.

Share correlation also refers to the relationship between stocks and other asset classes such as bonds, real estate, and more. In trading, correlation has many different applications, and much of what investors do is based on analyzing the relationships among various stocks and foreign exchange markets. The main benefit of trade correlation is to determine whether a relationship exists between variables and to understand the nature and strength of that relationship.

If the correlation is less than or greater than 1, something is incorrect in the calculation. A value of 0 means that the two variables are not correlated, and the relationship cannot be determined. When variables are correlated, it is useful for investors to understand how strong the correlation is, and whether it is a positive or negative one.

Correlation evaluates the relationship between variables and the various factors that influence that relationship. It is used when variables have a linear relationship with each other. Using scatter plots, we can examine the relationship between variables to determine whether they are correlated.

Causation may be a reason for correlation, but it is not the only possible explanation. The most commonly used direct measurement of diversification is correlation.

Correlation tends to weaken when taking a long position in one stock and a short position in others. Initially, it may appear that stock A is correlated with stock C, and everything aligns. If the correlation then returns to the observed mean or average, a profit may be realized.

In investing, correlation is a measure that indicates how two assets relate to their average prices. The correlation between asset classes can be measured by taking the long-term monthly return of one asset class and comparing it with another. A correlation coefficient of 1 indicates a perfect positive correlation between the prices of two stocks, meaning they move the same amount in the same direction.

Correlation should be measured over a period of months, years, or even days to understand how often two or more stocks move together. In pair trading, you can observe when price movements are correlated and tend to move in parallel. An investor can get a sense of whether stocks are related by examining whether a stock consistently outperforms or underperforms the average return over time.

Stocks in the same sector tend to have a stronger correlation than those in unrelated sectors. The purpose of studying market correlation coefficients is to understand how the market is likely to move. The best way to use correlation tools is to assess the specific risk of an asset class.

Correlation, sometimes associated with regression analysis, determines how dependent and independent variables are related. By dividing the covariance of the two variables in question by the product of their standard deviations, the calculated correlation coefficient reveals how likely assets are to move together within a portfolio. The formula used to calculate the correlation coefficient is the Pearson correlation coefficient (PCC), a statistical method named after Victorian mathematician Karl Pearson.

Portfolio risk is calculated by measuring the risk of a single investment as the standard deviation from the actual return of the portfolio over time. Since the correlation among investments shifts over time, higher volatility results in greater risk within the portfolio. Keep in mind that the correlation coefficient can change and reflects a shift in the portfolio's risk profile.

Diversified portfolios are built by investing in uncorrelated assets over time. When uncorrelated assets are included in a portfolio, they may be more volatile individually than correlated investments. However, diversifiable risks are reduced by managing the correlation coefficient between assets within the portfolio.

Another way to mitigate risk is to include assets that have little or no correlation with the stock market. Positively correlated investments are riskier because no single asset is guaranteed to positively correlate with another.

For example, an investment analyst may choose to investigate whether an asset will increase in value over time and whether it has a strong correlation with the stock market. The correlation coefficient is one of the factors to consider. The analyst may examine whether the investment is likely to grow in value and determine the strength of its correlation with the broader market.

In practice, an investor aiming to achieve returns that are independent of portfolio-wide risk could benefit from rebalancing into a lower-correlated asset class. If a stock investment delivers strong returns but is less correlated with another holding, hedging might reduce your overall returns.

Chapter 1 - Catalysts that Trigger Stock Prices Upwards and Downwards

Investors and buyers are constantly seeking out catalysts, as they represent a unique opportunity to benefit from significant price movements.

Catalysts are specific, noteworthy events that have real potential to temporarily drive down a company's share price over a short, accelerated period. There are eleven major catalysts that can move companies' share prices, although those prices might not always respond as quickly as expected.

For instance, when a company releases an earnings report, which is an official financial document issued by a business that outlines its expenses, profits, and overall income, and the results differ from expectations, this serves as a stock catalyst that can move prices. If a stock misses its profit expectations, it may not miss by as much as the market anticipated, but it can still impact pricing.

In equity markets, a catalyst refers to new information or an event that influences the price of a financial asset. A stock catalyst, also known as a news catalyst, is something with the potential to shift the stock price. Catalysts can also be indirect, such as government regulations that affect an entire industry.

It can be difficult for new investors to understand why the stock market rises or falls in percentage terms. However, becoming familiar with the different types of market catalysts can lead to a better understanding of how the market moves.

The forces behind large market movements are known as catalysts. Major developments in the stock market can lead to drastic shifts in current stock price trends. Financial and media-related catalysts can also bring about significant changes in these trends.

Simply put, a stock catalyst is any piece of information that triggers a dramatic movement in a company's stock. Examples of such catalysts include earnings reports, product announcements, press releases, CEO comments, or the passage of legislation by Congress.

Without a catalyst, bad news can rattle investors and disrupt upward momentum, while good news can leave a stock stagnant.

While catalysts are important for short-term direction, overvalued companies often remain overpriced until specific events, such as earnings reports or revised expectations, bring the reality into focus. If a company is high quality, undervalued, and has strong growth potential, its share price may rise over time even without a specific event. As noted above, whether or not an event becomes a stock catalyst depends on the context in which it occurs and the stability of the company.

If you're a long-term investor focused on value stocks, you're less concerned with trading on catalysts than day traders. Value investors like to see price changes as a response to catalysts because the movement aligns with their previous assumptions. For example, they believe the value of a company increases when the share price rises in response to a catalyst.

Either way, it is worth understanding what market catalysts are and how they affect both the market and the price of a security. There are several long-term catalysts that can influence the market over an extended period. One of the most important long-term catalysts is interest rates.

When the Dow Jones Industrial Average and the S&P 500 make large moves in a single day, financial media often attribute the cause to market catalysts. However, beginners may not have a deep understanding of what a catalyst truly is. In reality, the actual reason behind a market correction or plunge might not be one of the typical top ten catalysts, and we cannot predict the future with certainty.

Instead of waiting for a flood of developments, sometimes just a few key messages can act as catalysts. There are two or three potential catalysts that could drive a change in share price over the next 6 to 12 months.

Catalysts are specific key events that can lead the market to recognize price inefficiencies within the next 6 to 12 months, which may result in a price correction and the opportunity to generate profits.

Catalysts are situations that move stock prices over time, based on specific milestones. For instance, if a stock falls below its moving average or key support or resistance levels, it may have a catalyst that influences its price.

A strong catalyst may also trigger increased trading volume, a significant short squeeze, or a shift in a stock with a small float. Drastic price fluctuations caused by major stock catalysts can lead to heightened volatility.

Hard catalysts refer to news that is directly related to a specific stock. In contrast, soft catalysts are influenced by a company's external environment and have the ability to impact its share price. Stock catalysts usually affect companies in industries that are among the largest in the world.

In some cases, stocks in a portfolio are tied to catalysts that drive earnings growth, such as new product launches or corporate restructuring. In fact, mutual funds, often referred to as go-to value funds, apply a form of catalyst or milestone-based investing by buying or shorting shares. Some share catalysts influence companies in sectors that are among the biggest globally.

Share values can trade within seconds, so it's essential to have the most up-to-date information regarding price movements, chart patterns, and volumes. Look for equity research tools that offer real-time market streaming and charts. To find the best stocks to buy and watch, check out the IBD Share List and other IBD content.

The price-to-earnings ratio (P/E) is a popular measure of how expensive a stock is compared to others in the broader market. A lower ratio is generally more attractive than similar valuations. A stock with a high P/E can still be justified, while a low P/E stock may be a bargain. However, it's important to consider other financial metrics as well, such as price-to-sales ratios and the book value of assets and liabilities.

High-frequency trading, in which computers run programs that trade hundreds of shares in nanoseconds, can cause significant fluctuations in stock prices due to a wide range of macro and obscure factors. All stock sectors have their own quirks. For example, financial services companies typically trade at 14 times earnings, while technology companies trade at 24.

News can shake the share price of a particular company or an entire sector. Search for "CEO resigns when stock falls" and you'll see countless examples of share prices plummeting after a CEO resigns or is fired, causing the company to suffer.

The right catalysts can lead to increased volume or short-term bottlenecks for stocks with limited float. Catalysts can also be indirect, such as government policies impacting the Robinhood app for Windows 10 or E*TRADE being seen as the top stock in its industry.

It's important to determine whether potential catalysts are already reflected in the share price. When analyzing a company and making valuation estimates, it's often overlooked that catalysts are not always priced in. These catalysts are rarely reflected in stock prices, leaving non-algorithmic investors with little time to act on rising or falling trends.

A catalyst is an event or situation that moves the share price over time based on certain milestones. Today, I'll give you an introduction to stock catalysts and provide some concrete examples.

A stock catalyst is information that can affect the share price. It's also referred to as a news catalyst or simply a catalyst that has the potential to move the price.

There are countless factors that can cause the stock market to move in one direction or another, including economic data, geopolitical events, and market sentiment. During a trading day on the US stock market, you may notice certain patterns based on the time of day, although some periods may not follow any trend. Occasionally, major news events disrupt these patterns, leading to sharp reversals or significant movements during lunchtime. At other times, unusual external catalysts may influence the market.

A share split gives management confidence in the share price, which can trickle down to investors. While the split itself doesn't directly affect the stock's value, the circumstances surrounding it can influence price movement, either as a positive or negative catalyst. It's also important to understand that a reverse stock split can occur, and if it's perceived negatively, investors might still drive the share price up due to speculation or other factors.

Many companies and their boards of directors have split their shares throughout history to maintain an acceptable share price. A share split alters the number and structure of a company's outstanding shares. The primary benefit of a stock split is that it makes shares more affordable for smaller investors.

The imbalance between the supply and demand of a stock causes the share price to rise until equilibrium is reached. A higher share price results when more people want to buy the stock. If demand for a share increases, the share price can be expected to rise.

Share prices can spike or crash in a short period of time. On the other hand, tax increases may reduce the amount of money investors can allocate to the stock market, which negatively impacts a company's share price by leaving less capital available for investment.

Investors who believe a company can grow its earnings over the long term, and see the stock as currently undervalued, are often willing to pay higher prices despite short-term market trends. In these cases, the share price often rises after the company's ex-dividend date, followed by a slight decline.

Trading large blocks of stock in an illiquid market can cause significant price fluctuations. A liquid market, on the other hand, means low volatility and minimal changes in share prices, as there are enough buyers and sellers on both sides. When there are more buyers than sellers, share prices tend to rise because increased demand draws attention to the stock.

When a stock opens higher but closes lower, it creates a gap on the chart. Although this is not necessarily a pattern, it can be significant in the market. When a stock deviates from the prevailing trend in the opposite direction, it often signals a reversal.

Charting patterns, technical indicators, news catalysts, and countless other methods help traders identify opportunities. These tools show when and where to enter or exit a trade. A stock or a sector can surge or tumble in response to new information.

Stock catalysts are events or news that affect share prices. They can impact a single company, an entire industry, or the global market. Catalysts may involve negative headlines that unsettle investors or positive announcements that lift a struggling stock.

Much ink is spilled over daily stock price fluctuations because many people try to profit from short-term moves. However, long-term investors should focus on whether a company can grow earnings over several years. The decisive factor is whether the company can endure for five, ten, or twenty years.

A stock split occurs when a business divides its share price into smaller parts, making the company's shares more accessible for the average investor. This often increases demand, which can push the share price higher.

A share is a stake in a company that investors buy or sell through a bidding process on an exchange. For example, an investor might offer 10 dollars for a stock. The first published trade could occur at 10.10 dollars, where investor B buys from investor D. Then investor E might list the stock at 11.20 dollars but sell to the next lowest bidder, investor F, who is willing to pay 10.20 dollars.

You can use various factors to determine when to sell a stock. Multiple catalysts in the market can spark rapid price increases, and any extra information made available to investors can help someone profit in a short time.

There is also a long-term trend across the stock market. Buying behavior is often more pronounced with cyclical stocks. If you buy Tesla shares with the expectation that short-term fluctuations will eventually give way to a stronger long-term trend in your favor, that trend is currently robust.

Rational investors understand that stock price movements, as measured by the Standard & Poor's 500 Index, often reflect changes in expectations for the future. As a result, equity market returns may diverge from investor sentiment, because they magnify shifts in that sentiment. Since future prices are a proxy for these expectations, we can consider how policies and numerical data influence them.

There are catalysts in the stock market that can lead to drastic shifts in current share price performance. The most direct way to influence stock returns is to alter expectations, and the most practical method is often to reduce policy rates. This seems to be the only realistic step governments can take to change expectations and support higher share prices.

A catalyst is a specific event with the real potential to push a company's share price down or up for a relatively short but sustained period. In equities, a catalyst is also called a news catalyst because it can move the share price. Below are 11 well-known catalysts that may change a company's share price, although not always as quickly as some investors expect.

For traditional value investors, a catalyst can be a positive surprise if their assessment of the company is correct. It gives them a chance to increase their position if the share price dips, or to realize the value they anticipated if the price rises. Depending on the type of catalyst you are analyzing, the share price can rise or fall. A strong catalyst can lead to higher trading volume or a significant short squeeze in stocks with a small public float.

Chapter 2 - Catalysts that Trigger ETFs Prices Upwards and Downwards

From October 15, 2020, market prices and returns will be based on the official remaining fee of each ETF share. However, this fee will not be available at the midpoint of the nationwide best bid and the nationwide best offer at the time the ETF is calculated. Instead, it will be based on the current NAV per share. Shares in ETFs are bought and sold at market prices, not NAV, and cannot be redeemed by the ETF. These funds are sometimes accused of being speculative and driven by commodities.

Because ETFs are designed to track the value of an underlying asset or index (whether it is a commodity such as gold or a basket of stocks such as the S&P 500), the market prices of ETFs can differ from their underlying indexes. For a simple vanilla ETF that tracks a common index of listed securities in a developed market, such as an S&P 500 fund, the ETF's NAV and its market price tend to be nearly equal. However, many securities, and the ETFs that hold them, can change in value. As a result, the price you pay for a share in an exchange-traded fund may vary from its NAV.

There is some evidence that oil ETFs might have little effect on prices, but this is difficult to estimate because these ETFs do not exist in a vacuum, and investors can access various oil vehicles through futures contracts. Commodity exchanges and trading notes (also called ETNs) attract investor interest in commodities, but they have had no direct impact on prices, making it unlikely that these kinds of investments affect commodity prices.

Although ETFs trade like stocks, they function more like mutual funds or index funds, which differ in their underlying assets and investment objectives. While a stock represents a single company, an ETF represents a basket of stocks. Exchange-Traded Funds (ETFs) are funds traded on an exchange just like stocks, meaning they can be bought and sold throughout the day. Unlike stocks, ETFs have their own ticker symbols so investors can track their price activity.

ETFs have grown rapidly in recent years. They have been a popular investment vehicle for those seeking to secure precious metals. Last week, the Silver iShares SLV fund, one of the most heavily traded funds on certain platforms, was particularly strong. Some major hedge funds switched their exposure from gold futures to ETFs during the recent volatility.

Tesla's stock fell in 2020, leading to price disruptions that created attractive trading opportunities. This made Tesla an important catalyst for the recent rise in the price of gold. Gold holdings in exchange-traded funds give investors the chance to influence gold prices without physically owning or storing the metal, which has risen to 3,365 dollars per tonne this year.

For pure value investors, these catalysts can be welcome surprises if their assessment of the company is correct. They offer opportunities to build a position when prices fall and realize value when prices rise. The eleven best-known catalysts that move a company's share price may not always shift the price as quickly as anticipated. The tendency to buy is especially sensitive to cyclical stocks.

Depending on the catalyst you are reviewing, the share price can go up or down. Key developments in the stock market can result in drastic changes to a stock's current price trend. In stock markets, a catalyst is an event or announcement that drives up the price of a security. Catalysts are specific occurrences that can push a company's share price up or down over a short but heightened timeframe. Mergers and acquisitions, for example, can boost the share price of both the acquiring and the target company.

Higher demand for a company's shares pushes its share price upward. Stock splits increase a company's liquidity and trading volume. They also make the company more affordable for the average investor. Tesla's stock has a notable chance of rising next month, according to our machine learning model that analyzes five years of price data. This follows a 22% drop in the past five days.

According to the Trefis Machine Learning Engine, which identifies trends in corporate share price data over the last decade, Tesla shares have a strong 69% chance of rising next month after falling 12% in the last five trading days. The model shows that Tesla tends to return an average profit of 1.7% per month over 21 trading days, even after experiencing a 17% decline in the previous 21 trading days. You can test this with various other combinations of the model to see whether Tesla might rise or fall.

I understand that ETFs trade the same stocks each day, but I am unsure what drives their prices. Buyers and sellers trade ETFs daily, just as they do stocks. Price movements attract investors, and all ETFs follow the same flow pattern.

Chapter 3 - Factors That Trigger Stock Price Instantly

Investors need to consider stock price patterns and form an opinion about market trends they observe over a short period, especially when stock prices are volatile. When examining long-term price patterns, it is crucial to identify and define trends. If you want to understand stock market trends, you must learn the language of the market.

During a stock market trading session, several factors can affect a share price, including earnings reports, company news, economic data, and unexpected events that can impact an entire industry, sector, or even the whole market. If investors are aware of the most frequent market movements and the factors that influence stock prices, they can make better entry decisions and potentially gain an extra one or two percent in returns. Demand factors affecting stock prices include corporate developments, economic conditions, industry trends, market sentiment, and even unforeseen events such as natural disasters.

When the demand for a stock exceeds the supply of sellers, its price rises. However, stock prices fall when supply surpasses demand and more investors begin to sell.

The price declines when sellers of a particular stock exceed buyers. Investing in stocks is not risk-free, but it is a disciplined approach and one of the best ways to build wealth. This insight explains why people can make money in the stock market, but it does not account for the ups and downs that occur. Many factors can move the market in one direction or another, including economic news, geopolitical events, and market sentiment.

Companies, stocks, and their prices can be affected by global events such as war, civil unrest, natural disasters, and terrorism. Although news about a company may be anticipated, unexpected developments can cause sudden movements in its share price. Other factors, including wars, major corporate hacks, changes in federal laws and regulations, and natural disasters in productive regions, can also lead to significant declines in the prices of many stocks.

When an online author or journalist posts a bullish or bearish article about a company during a trading day, it can have a significant impact on the stock. It is important for investors to monitor stock movements and global news so they can stay in tune with the market.

For much of the trading day, there is usually an immediate imbalance between supply and demand for a stock, causing its price to move throughout the session. Price movements can be drastic if significant developments occur at a company. News about a specific business can shift its share price in response to perceived risk, and different investors with varying capital may receive the news at different times and set stop-loss orders, causing the share price to zigzag.

For example, if a buyer offers a lower bid at some point in the day, a trader may step in and attempt to resell the stock at a higher asking price, resulting in a small spread. It is important to track what happened if the stock was purchased at 1:00 pm at a lower price than at 11:00 am, because it affects entry and exit points. The most recent trading price is not always the current one. For less liquid stocks, the last trade can occur minutes or even hours before, allowing the market time to move and the share price to change quickly.

Fading is when investors sell a stock and buy it back later when interest wanes. Spread trading is a high-speed strategy that aims to capitalize on short-lived market sentiment by exploiting the difference between the bid and ask prices of a stock.

Think of the stock market as a large auction where traders bid for each other's stocks while also offering their own shares for sale. It might seem that anyone can buy or sell any number of shares at the current price at any time, but remember that in this scenario, more people want to buy shares than sell them.

Many individuals and organizations have an interest in promoting a particular stock or company to increase the value of their own holdings or profits. Positive economic reports, stock market newsletters, blogs, press releases, and news articles can build high expectations for a company's performance and push its stock price higher. Investors who believe a company can boost earnings over the long term and see the stock as undervalued may be willing to pay a higher price now due to short-term trends.

The price of an index is influenced by the same economic events that affect the stock prices of the companies that make up the index. When a currency falls, it can prompt investors to anticipate the ripple effects from a drop in the supply and demand for various products, services, currencies, and other investments in a country, creating a price-pull dynamic.

Chapter 4 - Factors That Trigger ETF Price Instantly

These necessities may change because of market volatility, the price fluctuations of ETFs, concentrated positions, the buying and selling of illiquid or less expensive securities, and other factors. Exchange Traded Funds represent an investment that mirrors the price and return of a given index. Investments are taxed differently: ETFs often incur fewer capital gains than investment funds, which are taxed when the ETF is sold to investors.

Some ETFs hold securities that can cause significant variations between market prices and NAV. Many securities in ETFs can change in value, so the price you pay on the market for a share in an exchange-traded fund may fluctuate from NAV. Some ETFs are bought, held, or sold by investors who purchase and hold them for asset allocation purposes, while others trade ETF shares to hedge risk or implement market-oriented investing strategies.

Because mutual funds and ETFs trade like securities, an investor can perform the same types of transactions as with a stock, including limit orders (to specify the prices at which they want to trade), stop-loss orders, margin buying and hedging strategies, and meeting minimum investment requirements.

Unlike mutual funds, exchange-traded funds (ETFs) are traded on an exchange. Unlike individual stocks, ETF shares trade throughout the day, and prices change according to supply and demand. ETFs can be bought or sold at any time of the day at the current market price, whereas mutual funds—being investment funds—trade only at the end of the day.

During the day, exchange-traded funds (ETFs) fluctuate when investors buy and sell shares. This flexibility allows shares of ETFs to be bought and sold at real-time prices throughout the trading day. Some ETFs permit intraday trading (unlike mutual funds) and also trade at closing prices.

Leading market makers and institutions buy and sell shares throughout the trading day, using ETFs as a pricing tool. Low-cost ETFs are managed by professionals who trade stocks that reflect the underlying benchmark, resulting in lower annual fees than those of actively managed funds. ETFs can trade like equities, allowing investors to use strategies such as selling short and buying on margin.

Another advantage ETFs share with other index funds is that they may be more tax-efficient than mutual funds because they do not sell securities to cover investor redemptions.

Unlike bond funds, ETFs can be used to reduce risk in a portfolio by diversifying investments and generating returns when the stock market reverses. The securities in a portfolio that includes an ETF can vary in value if the ETF shares, in exchange for open-ended investment funds managed under the same strategy, rise or fall. A plain vanilla ETF, such as one tracking the S&P 500, will have a net asset value (market price) that closely matches the index.

The spread between an ETF and the higher market price per share may or may not align with the intraday value of the underlying assets at any given moment. Some ETFs may trade at a premium above the Intraday Net Asset Value (INAV) or at a discount below INAV.

Investments in funds are subject to investment risk, including the possible loss of capital. Because the Fund is not actively managed, it cannot sell securities or remove them from its respective index, and its performance may differ from that of its index due to transaction costs, fees, and other factors.

ETF units are not redeemable and can only be issued and redeemed by the Fund if their net asset value (ANAVA) exceeds a certain block of shares designated as a creation unit.

An ETF is a basket of securities whose shares are traded on an exchange. Exchange Traded Funds (ETFs) are securities that replicate an index of commodities, bonds, or another investment basket (an index fund), much like investment funds. ETFs trade like stocks, each with its own ticker symbol, with investor capital contributing to a pool of funds that invest in particular assets.

When we think about ETFs that can be bought and sold on an exchange in real time, the first example might be an international equity fund or ETF (or, in the case of emerging markets, a relevant example). Thanks to exchange-traded funds, investors can buy and sell these kinds of assets at very low cost, enabling them to navigate large intraday market volatility without compromising their portfolios. Consider an International Equity Fund (ETF) or an Asian Security ETF: these may be listed on a stock market that is closed while we sleep.

More than 1,200 stocks, including many of the most popular ETFs, were halted on major exchanges after the Dow Jones Industrial Average dropped more than 1,000 points in a single day on August 24, 2015. Beware of strong bullish moves or reversals in the market if early trading happens to be in your favor. Although an ETF can experience less volatility than some investments, this does not mean it carries less risk.

For instance, if you sell an ETF share on the same day that you attempt to buy a traditional open-ended investment fund, you may find that your broker will not allow the trade. An arbitrage opportunity arises when demand for an ETF increases or decreases, as market prices or liquidity concerns prompt investors to create additional ETF shares. There are also predictable news events during a trading session that can drive the market in both directions.

Chapter 5 - The Fundamental Difference Between Stock Investment And ETF Investment

Because ETFs maintain the underlying assets of a stock, traders can buy shares from ETFs, including mutual funds, and because ETFs are more streamlined to trade, they can be traded through online brokers and do not require a full-service broker or a purchase from an investment fund company. ETFs may be bought and sold like regular stocks on an open market, unlike mutual funds, whose price is set at the end of the day.

Since ETF transactions include a broker fee, the traded stock is paid for by the investor. Because ETFs are traded daily, the current market price of the stock can be lower than the NAV. When deciding between ETFs and index funds, compare the fund expense ratio, as it is the ongoing cost you pay over the life of the investment.

You also pay a fee if you buy or sell shares, and ETFs are no exception. If you put a small amount of money into an ETF, such as a 200-dollar paycheck, the commission fees may be prohibitive. Some of the returns on an ETF may sound like a lot of money, but remember that the fund has hundreds, if not thousands, of other investors, and you are sharing profits with the company.

Because ETFs are traded like shares, they may be a less volatile alternative than buying and selling shares in individual companies over the long term. You can use ETFs to diversify by investing the money you would normally use to purchase the same stocks. It is safer to invest in a portfolio of various types of ETFs, because if one part of the market falls, you can invest in another segment.

Many mutual funds and ETFs use a covered call strategy to reduce volatility, simplify the covered call process, and provide a cost-effective way to offset portfolio allocations by investing in cash. Index funds and Index ETFs offer instant diversification of your portfolio and help protect it from market downturns at lower cost. They are managed passively, meaning the investment fund is based on an index that represents a subset of the broader investment market.

Over the long term, passive investment vehicles such as exchange-traded funds (ETFs) and index funds outperform the vast majority of active funds and are a good choice for most investors. ETFs and equities are similar in that they can represent high, moderate, or low risk based on the assets held in the fund and the associated risk of those assets. Investing in an index fund or ETF that mimics the S&P 500 does not protect you from losses, but it does reduce the risk and volatility you might face if you held certain individual stocks.

Most ETFs are not actively managed but are designed to track an index. Actively managed ETFs allow managers to select investments linked to a benchmark index at their discretion. Low-cost ETFs, managed by professionals, trade shares that reflect the underlying benchmark and have a lower annual expense than actively managed funds.

The biggest difference between ETFs and mutual funds is that ETFs are traded throughout the day, whereas mutual funds and index funds are bought and sold at prices set at the end of the trading day. You can buy or sell shares in ETFs on the stock exchange throughout the day, while mutual funds are priced at the end of the day. ETFs (and index funds) are excellent for long-term investments because ETF investors have the ability to buy and sell all day.

Unlike a mutual fund, which fixes its trading price each day at the close of trading, an ETF can be bought and sold throughout the day. Unlike individual stocks, ETF shares are traded continuously in accordance with supply and demand. While stocks focus on one company, ETFs track an index, commodity, bond, or basket of securities.

Stocks are a single instrument, but an ETF is a basket of different assets such as stocks, commodities, bonds, and other securities. An ETF manager buys these securities to create what is called a basket fund. Shares of these investments are then sold to investors through the fund manager.

A key difference between ETFs and mutual funds is that an active index investor can buy and sell ETF shares on an exchange with other investors. Unlike mutual funds, ETFs trade as securities in which the investor can perform the same types of transactions as with stocks, including limit orders, stop-loss orders, margin buying, hedging strategies, and meeting minimum investment requirements. ETFs can also track index funds that are similar to traditional mutual funds but trade on an exchange like regular stocks.

Instead of trading individual stocks, investors can choose from hundreds of mutual funds and exchange-traded funds (ETFs), which give them access to every corner of the financial market. ETFs offer many of the benefits of an investment fund, including diversification, and can be traded like stocks on an exchange such as the NYSE or Nasdaq. If you are an equity investor, you make decisions about where your money goes and which companies you invest in.

In a world of opportunities for stocks, ETFs, and Treasuries, it is in investors' best interests to understand their options. Exchange-Traded Funds (ETFs) are investment funds that trade shares on an exchange and not the shares of individual companies. ETFs require a professional to manage the investment, but you can still invest in stocks without needing a traditional broker.

ETFs, unlike mutual funds, trade as securities in which the investor can perform the same types of transactions as with stocks, including limit orders, stop-loss orders, margin buying, hedging strategies, and meeting minimum investment requirements. ETFs are bought and sold at the market price during the trading day, whereas mutual fund units are traded at the end of each trading day. Since ETFs can buy and sell shares throughout the day, mutual funds can only be purchased at the end of the trading day based on a calculated price.

One of the main differences between ETFs and mutual funds is that active index investors can buy and sell shares on an exchange along with other investors. Another key difference is that ETFs are traded throughout the day, while shares in mutual funds and index funds are bought or sold at the price set at the end of the trading day. ETFs (and index funds) are excellent for long-term investment because ETF investors have the opportunity to buy or sell throughout the day.

Instead of holding individual shares, investors can choose from hundreds of mutual funds and exchange-traded funds (ETFs), which offer them access to all corners of the financial markets. If you invest your assets conventionally in stocks, indexes, and bonds, ETFs adjust the allocation according to changes in your risk tolerance and goals. Once you have defined your investment objectives, ETFs can be used to gain exposure across industries and sectors in markets around the world.

You can use ETFs to diversify by investing money you would otherwise use to buy individual shares. For example, buying shares in a Technology Sector ETF is less risky than buying shares in a single technology stock because the ETF owns shares in many different technology companies. ETFs allow you to invest in the entire basket of shares that the ETF holds.

Investment funds (ETFs) are investment companies registered with the SEC that provide investors with a way to put their money into a fund that invests in stocks, bonds, other assets, or a combination of investments, with the return being the fund's earnings. An ETF is a basket of securities that you buy and sell through a broker or exchange. Exchange-traded funds offer many benefits and can be used as an excellent vehicle to achieve an investor's goals.

Investment trusts and ETFs are in many ways similar, but which is the better long-term choice depends on whether the fund invests in equities or bonds, for instance. ETFs that invest in equities tend to be more liquid, while ETFs that invest in alternatives (for example, index funds or actively managed ETFs) mean that investing in the fund is based on an index representing a subset of the broader investment market.

Stock funds invest in shares, also called stocks, which are portions of ownership issued by a company to raise funds. ETFs, on the other hand, are tied to a specific market index.

Investing in individual stocks requires more research, as you are responsible for selecting the companies in your portfolio. The value of diversification is less significant than it would be if you were diversifying among many different companies. A single share in an ETF can be composed of many different investments.

Many mutual funds are managed by a fund manager or team that decides which stocks and other securities to buy or sell in order to beat the market and help their investors profit. Fund managers monitor the market carefully and use their investment experience and knowledge to maximize fund performance. Managed funds can have varying outcomes depending on their holdings.

Investment funds and exchange-traded funds (ETFs) are a combination of many specific assets and represent the most common form of diversification for investors. These types of funds allow you to invest in a diverse portfolio instead of a single security.

An ETF manager buys shares, commodities, bonds, and other securities to create what is often called a basket of funds. The fund invests a portion of its capital in corporate bonds, government bonds, and other fixed-income securities.

While most investment funds require a minimum investment, investors can buy as few shares of most ETFs as they wish. ETFs trade like equities, but investors can also use ETFs for certain strategies, such as short selling or buying on margin.

Investment funds and ETFs must invest at least one-fifth of their holdings in other types of securities, including those some investors consider volatile but not necessarily aggressive. In other specific situations, equity index funds and mutual funds can be cheaper than ETFs because investment funds may have tax-advantaged accounts, making their tax implications less significant.

Due to their longer disclosure cycles and the broader latitude given to active fund managers to select investments, investment funds can be affected by market fluctuations, as fund managers may shift investments at the right time and deviate from the intended fund strategy more than investors realize.

The price you pay for a share is determined by the stock market, where thousands of investors buy and sell shares in a company based on their perception of the company and its potential to provide a positive return on investment. The company's share price increases when the value of the owners' investments in the company rises.

The secondary purpose of the stock market is to give investors who buy shares the opportunity to participate in the profits of listed companies. An investor will realize a 50-% return on their investment by selling the stock if they buy shares at 10 dollars and the price rises to 15. One investment may suffer a loss in value, but that loss can offset the gains of others.

Asset allocation divides your investment portfolio into different asset classes such as stocks, bonds, and cash. It can be difficult to diversify when investing in stocks, especially if you do not start with a lot of capital. The easiest way to spread your investments across different asset classes is to invest in mutual funds or exchange-traded funds (ETFs) because they hold a larger number of stocks than other investment vehicles, making them more diversified than a single share.

Investment funds consist of a pool of money raised by multiple investors that can be invested in many different things, such as stocks, bonds, and other assets. Moreover, mutual funds offer a diverse mix of stocks and bonds, meaning that a single investor with a small amount of capital can own a portion of many companies. Investment funds are companies that pool the money of many investors and invest in securities such as stocks, bonds, and short-term debt.

Index funds are similar to mutual funds, a type of equity investment that diversifies your portfolio across multiple stocks. Investors in index fund accounts that invest in a 401(k) plan can choose equity funds based on market capitalization. When you buy an equity fund, you get a weighted average return on the companies in the fund, although the fund can become more volatile if you hold too few stocks.

Today, many investors choose mutual funds that pool the money of thousands of investors and invest in a variety of stocks and bonds under a professional manager. You do not have to research individual companies on your own or buy and sell shares to become an investor.

Many people think of investing as a way to score short-term gains in the stock market, but it is through long-term investments that most investors build wealth. To be a successful investor, you need to invest in stocks so you can achieve higher returns than other forms of investment. Value investing requires that investors remain invested for the long term, applying effort and research to stock selection.

This can help investors identify stocks that will allow them to build wealth over time by carefully examining the company's products, financial records, and future plans.

Equity funds are an excellent choice for investors who want to be aggressive but do not have the time or inclination to make investing a full-time endeavor. Investment fund investors have more options: hundreds of equity, bond, and money-market funds are available, enough to meet any level of risk tolerance, from conservative to speculative. Investors who prefer lower risk might consider money-market funds, as their principal is generally safer and they earn the current interest rate.

It is important to note that, of all the different types of investments we have covered so far, the stock market is the best place to invest small amounts of money for potentially large returns. Investing your money there can be the most straightforward way to earn money, and that is the market. As mentioned above, you can invest in stock indexes just as you do in stocks and options, but one of my most important takeaways is that you should invest in individual stocks.

There is always the potential to lose money if you invest in securities and other financial products. Investments such as stocks, mutual funds, and real estate all carry some risk, and one never wants to be forced to sell them in a time of need.

Investing is one of the best ways to grow your wealth, but if you choose a company in which to invest, it carries the risk of losing money. If you invest in an individual company, you run the risk that its share price will crash, and you could lose money. If you see the share price fall by 5 to 10% within a week, you might want to sell, so if you are risk averse, consider avoiding investing in individual businesses.

Diversification is crucial to any long-term investment strategy, and balancing your current investments with your individual company stocks can help you spread your risk. When you choose shares, understanding your entire portfolio mix will help you decide how much you want to invest. Calculate how your new investments fit into your overall portfolio, whether you invest in individual shares, index funds, or bonds.

Investing lets you take money you do not need to spend immediately and put it to work for you. This means investing in stocks can be ideal money that you may not need for at least the next five years. In the meantime, the money you invest in stocks and bonds helps companies and governments grow, and it earns you compound interest.

For those new to investing, there can be a lot of mystery surrounding exchange-traded funds (ETFs). It is true that investing in products you do not understand is risky, but ETFs can be a relatively secure investment. Although some investment products, such as certain ETFs, are riskier than others, it is important to know which funds provide stable returns and which may end up costing your nest egg.

Unlike mutual funds, ETFs can invest in a wide variety of securities, providing automatic diversification for shareholders. Indexed ETFs are funds that invest in exactly the same securities in a given index, such as the S&P 500, in order to match its returns over time. With low expenses, instant diversification, and the ability to invest in trending sectors at the click of a button, these funds offer investors numerous advantages.

I think mutual funds used to be much more popular when we started, and there has been more talk about ETFs and indices, etc. How comfortable are you with individual shares compared to index funds or ETFs? In the beginning of the discussion, we mentioned that your comfort level depends on your risk tolerance in the stock market. If you look at Cathie Wood's ETF, it is an investment fund I used to own, and you can buy it as an ETF.

Whether you are investing in individual shares, as we have done, or in an index fund or investment trust in your 401(k), the more control you have over your holdings, the more engaged you may become.

While most of our clients invest in the public market through low-cost mutual funds and exchange-traded funds, we view private market and non-exchange investments as an important means of diversification. We prefer private equity funds, which are baskets of holdings, over direct investments in a single company or sector. Exchange-traded funds are cheaper and carry less risk than individual shares, and a single fund can hold a diverse set of investments.

Funds can help form the foundation of a diversified portfolio and act as a first step toward sustainable investment in the market. Index ETFs invest in what fund managers call disruptive innovations, new products, and services that change the way the world works. Thematic exchange-traded funds (ETFs) allow you to invest in a variety of emerging trends and industries, including blockchain, cloud computing, clean energy, and cybersecurity.

Bloomberg Intelligence Senior ETF Analyst Eric Balchunas has recommended some options for investors who want to invest in the above-mentioned topics without using an exchange-traded fund. It is an excellent entry into the stock market for new investors. Do-it-yourself investors may be best served by investing in broad commodity funds where they do not need specific knowledge of a particular commodity.

Unlike more diversified funds, thematic ETFs are exposed to certain risks, such as a decline in multiple growth stocks in a given sector, a possibility that makes them riskier than a diversified fund like an S&P 500 index fund. If you are trying to play a hot trend using thematic ETFs, you may need to manage them yourself. However, if you typically invest in diversified index funds like the S&P 500, a passive approach might be a better strategy. Of course, there are fund managers who do an excellent job, and I am not trying to discredit them, but research shows that index funds and ETFs deliver better returns over longer periods than investment trusts.

Commodity risk: one important factor to consider when investing in equity and bond markets is that many variables affect commodity prices. The lack of correlation between commodities and standard equity or bond investments can be helpful in certain periods, but commodity returns can drag down an investor's total return in other periods.

Another way to invest in commodities is through an exchange-traded fund that invests in commodity futures contracts, which are agreements to buy or sell a particular commodity at a predetermined price at a specific time in the future. You can also invest in a fixed-income product whose returns are linked to a basket or index offered by an investment broker.

Most brokers offer robust screening tools to filter the universe of available ETFs based on various criteria such as investment type, geography, industry, trading performance, and fund providers.

You will find that the most popular ETFs have expense ratios lower than the average weighted fee ratio of comparable funds under management, so do not be afraid to explore.

The ideas of six investment experts range from Chinese companies in the battery and solar energy markets to private commercial real estate funds, healthcare funds, and the reopening of hedge funds. The first Vanguard ETFs on this list are VVs that track the CRSP U.S. Large Cap Index, which includes companies accounting for the top 85% of investable market capitalization. By the end of 2020, Vanguard Group Inc. had bought 71 million shares to become institutionally owned.

I have used my network of angel investors and venture capital funds to make some direct investments in technology and private companies, and to buy shares from existing investors.

The Roundhill Sports Betting & iGaming Index is designed to provide investors with exposure to the sports betting and gaming industry by delivering investment results consistent with the price and value evolution of the Roundhill Sports Betting & iGaming Index and the Abetz Indexa.

Chapter 6: The Pearson Coefficient and Quantum Strategy The English mathematician and statistician Karl Pearson is credited with developing many statistical methodologies, including the Pearson coefficient, the chi-square test, the p-value, and linear regression. While he devised a rigorous approach to the mathematics of the Pearson product-moment correlation (PPMC), it was Sir Francis Galton's insight that led to the modern concept of correlation and regression.

The Pearson correlation coefficient is a statistical measure that assesses the relationship or association between two continuous variables. We can determine the strength of the relationship between two variables by calculating the absolute value of the correlation coefficient. In bivariate analysis, the correlation measures the strength of the association between the two variables and the direction of this relationship.

The coefficient of determination is a measure of the degree of variation explained by the model (the correlation model). The coefficient of determination can be expressed as a percentage, such as between 3.6% and 0.36%, which represents the percentage of variance shared between the variables. It is also known as the correlation of the variance shared by the variables.

A statistic that measures the relationship between variables (for example, in finance and the investment industry) and indicates the strength of this relationship between the two variables and its direction is represented by the correlation coefficient.

Note that the correlation reflects the strength and direction of the linear relationship (top row), not the slope of the relationship (middle row) and other elements of nonlinear relationships (bottom row). The correlation can be calculated from one of the selected replicated samples, resulting in a correlation of 1.

However, extracting the correlation coefficients of two groups of stochastic variables under high-noise conditions is not trivial, and canonical correlation analyses often report worsened correlation values due to substantial noise contributions. The covariance of the two variables (and the covariance between them) is related to the Pearson correlation coefficient (PCC), which reflects a linear correlation between variables and ignores many other types of relationships and correlations. The Pearson product-moment correlation coefficient can be influenced by extreme values that exaggerate or diminish the strength of relationships, especially when variables are not uniformly distributed.

The value of a negative number indicates a negative correlation with the relationship strength, while the value of a positive number indicates a positive correlation with the relationship strength.

You can use the Pearson bivariate correlation test to determine the statistically significant linear relationship between continuous variables (such as weight and height) and to assess the strength and direction of that relationship.

As we have seen from the definition of the Pearson product-moment correlation coefficient, this measure captures the strength and direction of a linear relationship between two variables. A negative value of the correlation coefficient means that a change in one variable corresponds to a change in the other variable in the opposite direction, while a positive value indicates the same direction of change. The Pearson correlation coefficient (PCC) is the ratio of the covariance of the variables to the product of their standard deviations and becomes most notable when one normalizes the covariance so that the resulting value is 1.

On the other hand, when the correlation coefficient is negative, some variables are interconnected: if the value of one variable increases, the values of the others tend to decrease. A perfect negative correlation means that the two assets move in opposite directions, while a zero correlation implies no linear relationship. As already mentioned, a mathematical relationship does not necessarily indicate correlation.

This process is repeated multiple times until the empirical distribution is re-sampled, and Pearson correlation coefficients are used to approximate the sample distribution of the data. Pearson, referencing Bravais (1846), discussed what happens when the method for calculating correlation coefficients, which involves the product of moments and the mean set of products, cannot prove that it best fits the data.

Using advanced statistical techniques with Taylor expansion, he showed that the optimal value of the regression tendency of the correlation coefficient is calculated as the product of the moment of x and y and the deviation from the observed values of their respective averages for a number of pairs.

Share correlation describes the relationship that exists between two stocks and their respective price movements. It also refers to the relationship between stocks and other asset classes such as bonds and real estate. An investor can get a sense of how well two stocks correlate by examining whether one outperforms or underperforms the average investor's return over time.

In the context of investments, correlation is a measure that indicates the degree to which two assets move relative to their mean prices. It helps investors illustrate the relationship between variables when trying to understand the movement of an asset or when comparing a security with a benchmark index. If the correlation between two stocks is 1.0, their prices move in perfect parallel.

When one stock goes up while the other goes down, the two stocks have a strong negative correlation. Stocks with a correlation near zero suggest there is little to no correlation between them. A negative coefficient indicates that the negative correlation between stocks is strengthening and that when one stock rises, the other falls.

The correlation coefficient is a value that predicts the extent to which stocks move in relation to each other. It measures the relationship between two stocks and the strength of that relationship when they move in parallel. The correlation coefficient measures the historical relationship between two stocks and provides a guideline for their future relationship. However, it is only capable of predicting stock market or individual stock returns to a limited extent.

The correlation between two asset classes can be measured by taking the long-term monthly returns of a particular asset class and comparing them. For instance, from 1926 to 2013, the correlation of the U.S. stock market to the monthly yield on five-year Treasury bonds was studied. This represents a correlation between the risk of low-beta equities (the slowest return) and the lowest market average.

If instruments have a correlation of 1, they have an inverse relationship. Many advisers use equity correlation in advanced portfolio calculations, and equity correlation values range from 1.0 to 10. When there is a correlation between two variables, it is beneficial for investors to understand how strong the correlation is and whether it is positive or negative.

A correlation coefficient of 1 indicates a strong positive correlation between the prices of two stocks, meaning they move in the same direction and by the same amount. A value of 0 means the two variables are not correlated, and no relationship can be determined. A negative correlation is often referred to as an inverse correlation and represents variables moving in opposite directions.

Consider another example, this time with low-correlated assets. For instance, the most correlated securities might be shares and put options, where the value of put options increases when the stock price falls. A perfectly positive correlation means that when asset A shows an upward deviation, it yields a higher return than a downward deviation, while another asset (B) might yield less in a downward deviation scenario.

One tool we can use to reduce portfolio risk is to examine the correlation between our assets, including equity correlations. Using equity ratios can help you determine the level of risk you are taking and how to offset it. If one stock investment yields steady returns but is negatively correlated with another, you might purchase a hedge to mitigate your overall risk.

One way to determine the equity risk of your portfolio is to analyze your wealth creation based on your equity correlations. The correlations among certain variables in the stock market are crucial to investigate in order to understand the risk and return of an equity portfolio in finance. Beta is a common measure of how closely individual stock prices correlate with the broader market and exchanges.

The concept of negative correlation is crucial for investors and analysts considering adding new investments to their portfolios. The current negative correlation environment is favorable for institutional investors, as it allows stocks and bonds to hedge against each other and enables chief investment officers to increase equity allocations while managing portfolio risk. Investors and analysts should examine how stock movements correlate with the broader market and among themselves.

Using historical stock data from the S&P 500 Index and bond data from the 10-year Treasury note, Weisberger and PGIM Vice President Junying Shen found that the negative and positive correlation between equities and bonds depends on the macroeconomic context. The correlation is never entirely negative, nor is it unchangeable, the two researchers noted. Positive correlations are important for financial advisers and analysts in investing because they can be used in financial modeling to determine trends and relationships between variables.

Real estate and equities, for example, typically have a low correlation. Bond prices tend to correlate strongly with the stock market, and many investors use bonds to balance their portfolios and manage risk. When the negative correlation between stocks and bonds becomes positive, it may compel institutional investors to rethink their portfolios.

When building our portfolios, it is ideal to invest in stocks, bonds, ETFs, and other assets that do not correlate strongly. Hedging offsets the most correlated holdings in your portfolio to manage risk. From this perspective, correlation data confirms that equities and five-year T-bills are distinct asset classes with their own unique risks.

Chapter 7 - News is The Immediate Trigger Of All Asset Prices In The World

It takes as little as only one second for any news to change the direction of a stock chart.

Stocks tend to correlate more strongly with stocks in exceptional sectors during periods of extended volatility, such as during the 2008 economic crisis. International markets can also be less correlated in times of instability.

This decline in correlation shape means that the diversification benefits of exchange-traded equity REITs are large relative to the broader equity market, but they primarily attract investors with an extended horizon when they focus on short-term results. Tactical decisions are made using short-term market conditions, and these decisions are, of course, based on temporary (misplaced) assessments and correlations. For example, investors who view equity REITs as financial organizations may buy and sell them according to short-term trends relevant to banks, which spread over time without prior notice to other investors. Such poorly informed trading can cause them to be overvalued relative to real estate market conditions or to move in the opposite direction, causing the correlation to fall over a longer horizon.

For example, prior to 2011, the various sectors of the S&P 500 had 95-degree correlations, meaning they moved in line with each other. This made it difficult to select stocks from different sectors to increase portfolio diversification.

For instance, shares in the same industrial sector, such as banking or healthcare, are more likely to move in exactly the same direction and react in exactly the same way to the market. This correlation is not immediately obvious in your portfolio if you own stocks through mutual funds or exchange-traded funds. For example, suppose you own shares in an energy company and also purchase shares in an ETF that invests in several sectors, including energy.

Share correlation describes the relationship between two stocks and their respective price movements. It also refers to the relationship between stocks and other asset classes, such as bonds and real estate. The Stock Correlation Network uses share price data to analyze the relationships among different stocks listed on the stock exchange.

There is a linear relationship between the value of the normalized correlation coefficient of mutual information and the large deviation in the rank of stock pairs derived from these two measures. This suggests that there is a linear relationship between the values of mutual information and the normalized correlation coefficient and that there are significant differences in the ranks of stocks in each pair derived from these metrics.

The second type of relationship is the most crucial nonlinear correlation among stock pairs. The third type of relationship mentioned here is also important for nonlinear correlations between stock pairs. Examples of the third type of stock pairs with large correlation coefficients and small mutual information values include Kibing Group (616,636) and Anxin Trust (600,816) (Fig. 3e), as well as Fujian Cement (600 802) and Guihang Automotive Components (600523).

To address the problem of nonlinear correlation, I propose a novel framework for the development of equity networks that use mutual information. Numerical results show that mutual information is an effective approach to estimating the correlation coefficient, which measures the equity relationship when the stock market is subject to large fluctuations.

We develop two equity networks that use mutual information and Pearson correlation coefficients to study the topological properties of these networks. Using data from 280 stocks traded on the Shanghai Stock Exchange between 2014 and 2016 in China, we assess the effectiveness of the correlation coefficient compared to mutual information for measuring equity relationships. We calculated the Spearman rank correlation between the daily number of mentions of a company and the daily return on its stock and found that the correlation coefficients did not differ significantly from zero (mean correlation coefficient = 0.000, mean correlation coefficient = 0.002, W = 2.62, p = 0.784, Wilcoxon signed rank test).

Our findings suggest that increased interest in corporate news is associated with greater movements in a company's share price in the market. Since larger trading volumes are known to correlate with bigger moves in the price of the company's shares, the relationship between news and absolute returns is expected to mirror the relationship between news and transaction volume. In other words, our analysis provides evidence that interest in corporate news correlates with the price movements of company shares, regardless of the direction of those movements.

In this chapter, we examine the dynamics of the correlation between mass media news and new media information when published in the Chinese stock market. The correlation is stronger when the stock market performs well. We attribute the decreasing trend in dynamic correlation to the decline in media attention and the weak performance of the market in new media.

The correlation coefficients between the new versions of new media and the new variants of new media are generally higher (around 0.9 and significant at 0.01), while the correlation coefficients between the mass media and their new variants exceed 0.9 (significant at 0.11).

CT correlation between municipalities and metropolitan regions was compared to news groups and soccer behavior. The table below shows that the characteristics of news media can have both low and high correlations. In column 2 of the panel, the lag coefficient between the number of mass media news items and the number of new media news items is positive and significant, suggesting an autocorrelation between the daily number of new media messages and the mass media news that leads to more news in new media.

The results indicate that the correlation between news in mass media and information in new media becomes stronger when the coefficient for reprints is weak and when the market performs well. On the other hand, the correlation coefficient is 0.7 between mass media news and new media reprints, as well as between new media information and mass media reprints. This high correlation coefficient suggests that mass media pay more attention to a medium (reprint) of news than to other media.

Online calculators allow you to determine stock correlations, but you can also do the calculations yourself. For example, if you are a day trader examining daily returns on assets, you can estimate their correlation based on those daily returns. Since large trading volumes are known to correlate with big moves in a company's stock price, the relationship between news and absolute returns is expected to be similar to the relationship between news, transactions, and volumes.

The Stock Correlation Network uses share price data to analyze the relationships among different stocks listed on the stock exchange. In general, share correlation refers to how closely stocks move relative to each other. When we talk about asset classes being correlated, we quantify that correlation.

The fourth type includes stock pairs in which the mutual information correlation coefficient is low. We develop equity networks that use mutual information and Pearson correlation coefficients to examine the topological properties of these networks. There is a linear relationship between the value of the correlation coefficient between mutual information and the large variation in rank of the equity pairs derived from these measures.

Before you relinquish control of your investments to an advisor, it is a good idea to familiarize yourself with the fundamentals of equity correlation. Numerical results show that mutual information is a more effective measure than the correlation coefficient for assessing equity relationships when the stock market is subject to large fluctuations. Stocks tend to correlate more strongly with stocks in exceptional sectors during periods of increased volatility, as seen during the 2008 economic crisis.

Investors may want to include assets in their portfolios that have a lower market correlation than the stock market to manage risk. By investing in assets with low or negative correlation, such as stocks and bonds, investors can reduce their portfolio risk. International markets may still become more correlated even in times of instability.

By selecting different stocks, investors can diversify by investing in various types of assets. One common way to diversify a stock portfolio, for example, is to include bonds, which tend to have low correlation with stocks. Adding low-correlated stocks to your existing portfolio can help offset risk.

For example, real estate stocks are less correlated with each other. Bond prices often correlate strongly with the stock market, and many investors use bonds to balance their portfolios and manage risk. Some investors may view equity REITs as financial institutions and trade them based on short-term trends relevant to banks, but other investors may eventually notice these ill-informed trades, causing the assets to become overvalued relative to real estate market conditions or move in the opposite direction, which leads to lower correlation over a longer horizon.

This decline in the correlation structure means that the diversification benefits of exchange-traded equity REITs are greater than those of the broader equity market. However, compared to financial sectors, they attract investors with longer horizons when they focus on short-term outcomes. A value of 1 means that two stocks have a perfectly positive correlation. When one stock goes up while the other goes down, they have an almost perfect negative correlation (noting that this value is -1).

We calculated the Spearman rank correlation between the daily number of company mentions and the daily return on the company's stock and found that the correlation coefficients did not differ significantly from zero (mean correlation coefficient 0.000, mean correlation coefficient -0.002, W = 2.62, p = 0.784, Wilcoxon signed rank test). In other words, the daily mentions of the company's name did not correlate with the stock's daily returns. However, our analysis suggests that interest in a company is broadly correlated with its share price moves in the news, regardless of the direction of the interest.

To understand media coverage, we examine how it correlates with the geographical factors predicted by the gravitational model. In this model, we characterize the news focus as a function of population size and distance from the media source. As noted, we model media sources as the communities where the news station headquarters are located, based on the station's name.

Index funds traded on stock exchanges as Exchange Traded Funds (ETFs) are attractive to investors because of their broad diversification potential, the wide variety of different ETFs, the features of their underlying assets, their sectoral focus, and the many opportunities for benchmarking. Inverse ETFs that track the same index often show a high correlation between their price and their trading volume, suggesting they may be used to prevent the price of the underlying asset from falling. On the other hand, high market correlation means that investors might opt to use simple index funds to participate in the market rather than attempting to select individual stocks.

One fund, a sector-oriented ETF that tracks the performance of US companies active in the financial sector, had the strongest positive correlation. There are many other types of mutual funds, including gold funds that invest in gold, gold funds that earn returns by investing in fixed-income government securities, and exchange-traded funds (ETFs) in which shares of various stocks are listed on the market and traded as a single share, as well as share-based savings plans (ELSS) that have a minimum three-year lock-in period during which investors cannot withdraw. This can be expressed as the median difference between quarterly and daily returns with the two (depending on the observed period of positive values known as a bear method) and the median yield differences expressed as a buy or inversion. Exchange-traded funds appear to be more profitable with smaller losses compared to short ETFs with the same index.

Investing through exchange-traded funds (ETFs) in frontier markets, which are countries and economies outside of developed and established emerging markets, is a good way to diversify away from US equity portfolios. Investors need assets in their portfolios that have a lower correlation with the stock market to manage risk. Bond prices often correlate with stock markets, and many investors use bonds to balance their portfolios and control risk.

The framework for forecasting and allocating funds by sector proposed in this section is derived from the approach used by portfolio managers who invest in equities over many different time horizons to maximize investor returns. Sector diversification, including the use of sector ETFs, can help reduce the risk of sector concentration associated with certain high-yield strategies. Correlation can be applied to individual securities, but for equities, it measures the overall market correlation, meaning how asset classes and the broader market move in relation to each other.

Owning a mix of stocks, mutual funds, bonds, and other investments can help protect your portfolio from inevitable periods of market volatility. ETFs that invest in multiple sectors, such as energy, can hold shares in the same or similar companies, which may overlap with your portfolio and increase your risk factors if you are overexposed. Individual investors may also choose mutual funds because they are managed by experienced, professional portfolio managers who can invest in multiple stocks across different sectors and mitigate risk factors.

To remain invested in the stock market, a diverse portfolio of mutual funds is a good option for many retail investors. Sector diversification, including sector ETFs, is an effective strategy for adapting to changing market conditions. For instance, suppose you own shares in energy companies and also purchase shares in an ETF that invests in multiple sectors, including energy.

Share correlation refers to the relationship between stocks and other asset classes, such as bonds and real estate. For example, two stocks in the same industrial sector, such as banking and healthcare, tend to move in the same direction and react similarly to the market. We have identified a large number of dominant ETFs whose returns are strongly correlated with those of cheaper and more liquid competitors.

Sectors contain many stocks that are tied to certain industries and often display strong correlations. Indeed, some sectors have a long history of divergent performance patterns.

Chapter 8 - Stock Market Crashes and Correlations

The 1929 Wall Street Crash, also referred to as the Great Crash, was a sudden and precipitous decline in stock prices in the United States in late October 1929. Other causes included an interest rate hike by the Federal Reserve in August 1929, as well as a moderate recession in the summer, which contributed to a gradual fall in stock prices in September and October that panicked investors.

The 1929 stock market crash, also called the Great Crash, was a sharp decline in US stock prices in 1929 that contributed to the 1930s' Great Depression. The main cause of the 1929 Wall Street crash was the long period of speculation that preceded it, during which millions of people invested their savings and borrowed money to buy shares, pushing prices to unsustainable levels. Investors began withdrawing their money from banks and mutual funds around the world because they did not know what would happen next, and they failed to suspend subprime and other non-performing loans.

Financial markets stopped functioning as everyone attempted to sell at the same time, and many institutions that needed new financing could not obtain it. The second likely cause was the strong expansion of mutual funds and public utilities, as well as the extent of margin purchases that fueled the acquisition of public utility shares and drove their prices higher. In 1929, the share prices of public utilities were more than three times their book value.

At the height of the summer of 1929, 300 million of these stocks had margins that propelled the Dow Jones Industrial Average to a record high of 381 points. US investors were not harmed by small amounts of Japanese stocks in their portfolios. Our UBS changed course and moved from investing in growth shares in February 2000, following guidance from UBS Brinson and its subsidiary Phillips Drew, just before the market peaked.

This indicates that while returns can be expected to mirror their asset classes, the selection of those classes is just as important as market timing for individual asset choice. Shrewd investors, for example, do not change their asset allocation based on the relative performance of one asset class but increase stocks in a portfolio when the stock market is hot. The reality is that many investors put money into multiple sectors, and asset classes are more prone to rising and falling than they should be.

Genuine portfolio diversification can be achieved by selecting and maintaining a broad range of asset classes, as well as through individual stock selection and market timing. Many investors do not realize how effective diversification can be, and they assume they can diversify by dividing their investments among large-, medium-, and small-cap stocks, energy, financial, health, and technology shares, and by investing in emerging markets. In this article, we show how to achieve true diversification by selecting asset classes, choosing stocks, and timing the market.

"If the stock market crashes, there will be enormous volatility that makes you wonder if the world is going to end tomorrow," says Terry Marsh, professor emeritus of finance at the Haas School of Business at the University of California, Berkeley. "Many commodities are failures, but if you own the right stocks that are cheap and do not move too fast, you can make a lot of money. So, I do not see the possibility of a correction in commodities. If the American stock market falls for a while, central banks will panic, print more money, and bring the market back up."

Here is an overview of eight of the most significant stock market crashes in recent financial history, along with their causes and effects. In 1929, there were three critical multipliers indicating that a change in the underlying value of a public utility led to a larger change in the stock market's price and in the value of investors. Most investment funds were not listed at the New York Stock Exchange when new closed fund options began, so stock prices reflected the selling pressure under which shares were offered at a discount to net asset value. In September 1929, most trusts that were not offered were discounted because inclusion involved bias.

As in the heyday of 1929-2000 and the 1950s of 1972, when second-tier companies were championed, today's markets exhibit extreme differences in value between asset classes, sectors, and companies. Bonds have traditionally been the most expensive relative to equities. The least expensive end is traditional securities around the world relative to growth stocks.

He added that investors now have time to watch the bigger picture and shape their portfolios to reflect how the stock market will perform over the next two to three years. An extended bull market can lead to an overweighting of an asset class that is due for a correction. The real issue with asset allocation remains in times when asset prices are below fair value.

The 1929 Wall Street Crash, also called the Great Crash, was a significant American stock market crash that occurred in the fall of 1929. The crash began in September and ended in October, when the New York Stock Exchange's share price plummeted. Because of the stock market crash that also occurred on October 29, 1929, it was referred to as the "great crash" or "flight of 29." It started on October 24 (Black Thursday) and lasted until October 29 (Black Tuesday), when the NYSE shares crashed. In the days leading up to Black Tuesday, there was widespread turbulence in the stock markets, panic selling, and high trading volumes, punctuated by brief periods of recovery.

The crash started on October 24, 1929, also called Black Thursday, when the market opened 1% lower than the previous day. Institutions and financiers stepped in to push up market prices to contain the crash, but losses on Black Thursday were modest, and shares rebounded over the next two days. The market closed six points higher as several major banks and investment firms repurchased large blocks of stocks in a successful attempt to contain a real panic on the first panic day, October 24. However, their efforts to support the market ultimately failed.

Other reasons included a Federal Reserve interest rate hike in August 1929 and a mild recession in the summer, which contributed to a gradual decline in stock prices in September and October, causing investors to panic. As values started to fall, investors panicked further and sold their shares. This led to an additional drop in prices, triggering a mass panic and stock sell-off that caused the crash of October 1929 and plunged the American economy into a depression.

Commercial banks continued to lend to speculators, while other lenders invested increasing amounts in loans to brokers. As stock prices soared during the Great Hoover Bull Market, public banks and tycoons rushed to brokers to invest their liquid assets: their savings and securitizations, which they could then sell for a profit. The market peaked on September 3, 1929, when the Dow rose to 381 points.

When investors used margin accounts to buy shares they could not afford, new money flowed into the stock market, driving up share prices. Margin purchases magnified profits and losses from price changes because they allowed people to make purchases without having the cash to back them. In 1929, so many people bought on margin that they accumulated debts amounting to six billion dollars.

It is a misleading view that the 1929 stock market crash was the only cause of the Great Depression, but the dramatic events of October did play a role in the decline of the American economy. The market's fall from its peak was so deep that it plunged the nation into an economic depression for more than a decade. The main cause of the crash was the long period of speculation beforehand, during which millions of people invested their savings and borrowed money to buy stocks, causing prices to become unsustainable.

Historians debate whether the 1929 stock market crash was the cause of the Great Depression, but there is no question that the crash affected the American economy for decades. Some argue that the 1929 crash triggered the Depression, but it coincided with the bursting of a loose credit-driven economic bubble. Only sixteen percent of American families were invested in United States stock markets in the pre-Depression period, suggesting that the crash alone has less weight in causing the Depression.

The bursting of the stock market bubble triggered a cascade of market forces that plagued the American economy in the years after 1929. The economy recovered in the following years, and the combined effects of excessive borrowing, business closings, and mass layoffs did not exacerbate or prolong the Great Depression. It was a prosperous decade, but the downturn that ended it was a recession beginning in the second half of 1929. Economies usually experience recessions every two to three years, but for some reason, the 1929 recession turned into a Great Depression.

In the years that followed, there was financial turmoil as the US economy contracted by more than 36% in terms of gross domestic product between 1929 and 1933. Many investors and ordinary people lost all their savings, and numerous banks and companies went under. Many US banks failed, causing their customers to lose their savings, and the unemployment rate rose to 25% as people lost their jobs.

The decade called the Roaring Twenties came to a dramatic and abrupt end with the stock market crash in October 1929, paving the way for America's Great Depression of the 1930s. The Hoover administration's promised "Great Crash" did not materialize when the market lost half its value in 1929, and many Americans were plunged into financial ruin. For many years, they endured the consequences of the 1929 Wall Street Crash, the most significant decline in American economic history. It wiped out savings, destroyed public trust, bankrupted banks and businesses, and led to numerous suicides and mental breakdowns, as well as damaged public services.

One of the worst declines in US history destroyed trust in the Wall Street markets and caused the Great Depression. The period before that, often referred to as the Black Thursday crash, was a time of extraordinary growth and speculative expansion. The apparent prosperity of the 1920s was real but proved limited.

The market reached a new low in November, but it was not until July 1932 that it hit the depths of the Great Depression, falling 89% from its peak. As a result of deflation, prices fell for more than a decade, from 1929 to 1933.

When stock prices slipped on October 29, people rushed to sell their shares on the market, driving prices down further. In the weeks that followed, share prices continued to decline.

Before the pandemic-induced market crash in March 2020, the US equity sector was behaving in an unusual way: high volatility and low correlation. This was, at least in recent decades, a departure from post-crash market behavior. The major world markets fell for more than a month, which was remarkable in itself. Indeed, this contrasted with the usual low correlation between countries' yields and the fact that world stock markets are more diverse than their companies.

It may be difficult to argue that the collapse of Southeast Asia's stock markets was the result of a bubble bursting, given that equity prices in these markets had been rising for six years before the 1997 currency crisis. However, price-to-earnings and price-to-book ratios suggest that, at the start of the crisis, Asian shares were not overvalued, implying that the crisis was not simply the result of a bubble popping.

Calvo and Reinhart demonstrated correlation changes associated with the Mexico crisis, and Baig and Goldfajn found an increased correlation between several East Asian markets and currencies during the East Asian crisis. This paper describes various theories about why co-movements in stock markets between countries became more important to investors after the crash, reducing the benefits of international diversification. The authors identified an increase in the correlation between stock returns during the 1987 crash in Bertero and Mayer, as well as in King and Wadhwani.

The crash was caused by the bursting of the price bubble, owing to the massive sell-off that ensued when most market participants tried to sell at the same time.

Stock prices began to fall in September and early October 1929, and the decline began on October 18. Investment companies and leading bankers tried to stabilize the market by purchasing large packages of shares, resulting in a modest rally on Friday. On Monday, however, a storm erupted and the market went into freefall.

Other causes of the 1929 stock market crash included low wages, runaway indebtedness in the battered agricultural sector, and the abundance of large bank loans that were not liquidated. The 1929 stock market crash was not the only cause of the Great Depression, but it accelerated the worldwide economic collapse of which it was a symptom. Although there is no consensus on the precise cause of the crash, evidence suggests that fear and speculation helped push the stock market closer to the brink of collapse. Some conclude that buying mutual funds on margin was the most likely factor causing share prices to drop, though there is no reason to conclude that margin buying caused the October market crash.

What happened after the crash makes for an interesting discussion regarding market correlations. Empirical results indicate a negative correlation between EPC and the risk of a stock market crash, suggesting that a tightening of EPC raises crash risk.

The strongest premise of the "Bitcoin is not correlated with equities" argument is that Bitcoin has its own market cycle, connected to a halving that appears to dictate its price movements, rather than external economic forces. This theory is based on so-called unwilling cooperation behavior, in which investors imitate other investors, leading to increased market cooperation and strong investor interaction. This translates into a greater rise in market prices in the months and years before the crash.

The study of financial contagion has advanced the notion of correlation breakdown, a paradigm that helps explain important dynamics in financial markets such as crises and asset bubbles. Investors measure the value of their investments, which is reflected in the share price, against the company's expected future cash flow. They adjust the fair value of this cash by a certain discount rate, under the assumption that a dollar is worth more today than a dollar tomorrow. Return volatility is the first and second moments of the return distribution, and we use conditional bias to measure the risk of a stock market crash, paying attention to the third moment of the return.

We note that conditional imbalances respond to changes in the rate of economic uncertainty, which suggests that reducing economic uncertainty lowers the risk of a stock market crash. Although there is no consensus on the exact causes of the 1929 to 1932 stock market crash, this text criticizes the arguments supporting several favored conclusions. It argues that standard macroeconomic reasoning is insufficient and that any strong and volatile regime change attributed to collective behavior (imitation and herding) should be considered, while also emphasizing a nonlinear dynamic view of the issues in order to understand the economy and stock markets.

Chapter 9 - Immediate Effect of Earnings Announcements and Sales Announcements

Stocks that have larger expected volume gains after an announcement (compared to the month beforehand) and higher awareness of past buying and selling activity after a profit declaration tend to experience more attributable purchases following the announcement date, mainly from smaller investors. At the same time, these shares tend to have higher follow-on rates.

Owen Lamont and Andrea Frazzini further demonstrate that the rates for earnings announcements correlate with the degree of trading activity around previous earnings releases, and that higher-volume shares around earnings announcements specifically have higher prices and greater implied purchases by individual investors. In line with the attention-grabbing hypothesis that individual investors are more likely to buy shares that draw attention due to a strong profit declaration, retail investors purchase first, leading to a surge in retail-initiated transactions on announcement days. After the declaration, there is also a high implied buyout by major investors.

If a company publishes an earnings report that does not meet market expectations, its share price can decline. The effect on share prices can also result from actual earnings that differ from consensus expectations, earnings surprises, or corrections to earnings estimates. With established stocks, there is ample time for a company to meet or exceed analyst expectations or to make a strong forecast and still see its share price fall.

Share prices are determined based on potential investors' expectations regarding a company's future profitability. This refers to the collective expectations of individual investors based on their assessments of fundamentals and market sentiment, rather than solely relying on published analyst forecasts. In the modeling era, share prices are based on estimates and expectations of actual outcomes by investors and analysts for a company's future profit and cash flow.

Quarterly results are valuable for those who use publicly available content from trusted journalists and analysts to remain informed about the companies in which they invest, and to base their investment decisions on new insights. Earnings calls are important because they have an immediate effect on stock prices. They provide information on how potential and current investors perceive the company and how this affects their investments.

You may have heard the terms "guidance" and "earnings call" used to describe how a company aligns analysts and investors with its forecasted future performance. These announcements are addressed to investors and are intended to influence the market. Whispers originate from corporate insiders, and cautious investors aim to manage the share price.

Several factors contribute to this trend, including cost ratios, distinct fund assets, shifting the burden of stock ownership from long-term investment funds, economies of scale, investor preferences, and competition among ETFs. Here are five aspects of stocks and ETFs that might surprise you. Many investors are familiar with Exchange Traded Funds (ETFs), which are traded on the market from open to close and mimic a basket of securities similar to an index investment fund.

Despite strong growth in financial and corporate earnings, the share price has fallen for a significant portion of the rally since March 2020, and the limited breadth of major indexes has been evident during much of that time. However, there has been a broad decline in the Nasdaq and Russell 2000 in recent months, as inflationary concerns have put downward pressure on highly valued segments of the market.

Studies suggest that stock prices consolidate when there are significant positive earnings surprises that indicate above-average performance, while negative surprises can exceed average performance. Long-term investors are not swayed by disappointing quarterly results, which some traders may consider short-term setbacks. Choosing positive-return stocks that surprise on earnings can be rewarding.

According to a 2009 study by financial analytics provider Intellibusiness EventVestor, companies that issued either positive or negative earnings forecasts in the first quarter of 2009 performed better than companies that did not issue earnings forecasts the following day. Dellinger and Pollet found that a trading strategy of purchasing shares of companies that made profit announcements on Friday, and selling shares of companies that released news on other days, yielded a monthly return that was four percentage points higher than expected, based on a standard stock price model.

Investor inattention to Friday earnings announcements, published in the Journal of Finance in 2009 by UC Berkeley economics professor and co-author Joshua M. Pollet, DellAvigna, and Pollet, indicates an underreaction to information as the cause of price fluctuations, pointing to investor distraction as the likely reason. The idea that factors like limited attention affect stock prices is supported by the assertion that financial models must account for psychological dynamics.

High opt-in rates allow Facebook to track user activity on third-party websites without impeding the delivery of personalized ads, which explains why FB's stock took a sharp downturn on January 28 following its large profit jump and a barrage of price-target increases of up to 360. In this scenario, investors reduced their appetite for the stock, resulting in a lower price-to-earnings ratio. This implies that it may not make sense to buy the stock after an initial drop due to a negative earnings surprise, as there is a strong likelihood that it will underperform the market for a time.

Stock market investors can determine a company's equity value by examining factors such as earnings, historical performance, future projections, and market share. The valuation ratio divides a company's market capitalization by the carrying amount of equity (earnings before net income) reported on the balance sheet and by turnover in the income statement. Valuation ratios that show how expensive a stock may be to investors include the price-to-book ratio, the price-to-earnings ratio, and the price-to-sales ratio.

The price-to-earnings ratio (P/E) is an important metric for evaluating the valuation of different companies. This ratio is used because of the recognized relationship between the share price, earnings per share (EPS), and corporate growth. Comparing the price-to-earnings growth ratio (PEG ratio), along with the P/E ratio and related metrics, helps determine how expensive a stock is by comparing its share price with its earnings.

The PEG ratio takes the P/E for shares and divides it by the expected annualized rate of earnings growth over the next few years to create a more level playing field. By considering growth, the PEG ratio helps investors compare a company's share price relative to its future earnings potential.

The forward P/E indicates how much shareholders are willing to pay for each dollar of a company's current earnings. The P/E ratio reflects the market's expectations of the price investors will pay for both current and future earnings.

A higher P/E suggests that investors expect the stock to grow and its share price to rise. Because investors pay one dollar for every dollar of corporate earnings, the P/E ratio is an important indicator of how much an investor is willing to spend for each dollar of the company's assets.

A P/E ratio of less than 1 suggests that the stock is undervalued because the value of the assets on the company's books is higher than what the market allocates to the company.

Investors and analysts use EPS (earnings per share) to compare the profitability of different companies. EPS shows how much a company earns per share, and a high EPS suggests that the stock has higher value relative to other shares in the industry.

It is calculated by dividing a company's total earnings by the number of shares outstanding. The lower the figure, the more you pay for the company's anticipated future earnings growth. This is divided by the company's net profit, i.e., by the number of shares outstanding.

The price-to-earnings ratio (PEG) is a company's share price divided by its annual earnings per share. It is calculated by dividing the P/E ratio by the projected earnings growth of the company.

The price-to-earnings ratio (PEG) is the share price divided by earnings per share, indicating how much investors pay for a company's profitability. It is a common benchmark in fundamental analysis and is useful for evaluating companies in the same industry that have comparable growth prospects. The Price Earnings-Relative (PEG) is another metric that helps investors value a stock by considering the market price, earnings, and a company's future growth potential.

A high P/E may indicate that the stock is overvalued relative to comparable stocks, especially if corporate earnings are not expected to grow as quickly. The P/E ratio is often used to evaluate mature, stable companies that are still profitable.

Companies with steady year-on-year earnings growth tend to outperform those with volatile earnings over time. If the share price does not deviate from earnings levels, the pattern of earnings growth helps demonstrate the company's stability and strength.

A key component in analyzing earnings reports is the company's earnings per share (EPS), which reflects total earnings divided by the number of shares outstanding. Earnings measure the money that a company makes and can be assessed on the basis of EPS, an important indicator of a company's financial health. Earnings are crucial in evaluating a company's profitability and are a major factor in determining its share price.

As you can see, there are countless metrics and indicators that investors can use to evaluate a company's overall financial health and determine the intrinsic value of its shares.

Before investing in a company, it is important to measure some of its key financial indicators. Both investors and lenders need to see a company's financial statements before deciding whether to invest or extend credit. Profit and loss statements contain several financial indicators that can help determine whether you should invest in the company.

Many business owners do not have a clear understanding of what their net earnings are, so this is a good starting point. Financial statements present a company's net earnings, which is the money left after expenses are paid. Unsustainable gains are detrimental, and losses can be acceptable if the company can eventually return to profitability.

Share investors can learn a great deal by examining a company's financial statements. A company's income statement, balance sheet, and cash flow statement are useful for understanding how the business operates, how stable it is, and how much its shares are worth. Stock investments require careful analysis of financial data to find a company's true value.

Wall Street investment firms, banks, loan officers, and informed business owners can analyze financial metrics to gain deeper insight into a company's current financial health and potential. Once you become familiar with these tools, you can transform the raw figures in your company's financial statements into information that helps you manage your business more efficiently. For example, debt-to-equity and debt-to-assets ratios can help bankers determine how your assets are financed and whether they come from lenders or from your own investments.

The current ratio measures your company's ability to generate enough cash to meet its short-term financial obligations. Another ratio indicates the firm's long-term solvency and the extent to which it relies on long-term debt to support its operations. The data used to calculate the inventory turnover ratio is taken from the company's income statement.

One of the most useful methods for small business owners to examine a company's annual accounts is to use the common-size ratio. This ratio transforms balance sheet data, such as having 12,000 in cash equivalents, into information about the percentage of total assets that are in cash. Another common analytical tool is the profitability ratio, a cross-sectional analysis that compares metrics across different companies in the same industry.

As we observe, Galectin Therapeutics has institutional investors holding a substantial portion of the company's shares. Institutional investors often consider investing in large companies included in relevant benchmark indexes. Keep in mind that this may depend on the size of the company's cash flows.

This implies that analysts working for institutional investors study the company's shares and favor them. Investors often use the S&P 500 index as a benchmark for stock performance, since it comprises 500 of the largest publicly traded US corporations. Investors may want to use this index as a benchmark for stocks because it is a reliable gauge of large companies.

Fund companies use benchmarks to measure the performance of a portfolio and its investment universe. Portfolio managers choose a benchmark that aligns with the fund's investment universe. Institutional investors compare their own returns with the returns of these benchmarks.

Benchmarks, risk metrics, and monitoring enable investors to identify opportunities to rebalance portfolio investments and capture market opportunities. The use of index-based investing or passive fund-specific portfolio allocation is one of the most advanced applications of benchmarking. Research, data collection, and analysis by companies, advisors, executives, investment managers, brokerages, and corporate issuers provide detailed peer-to-peer comparative analyses throughout the year.

Our executive rankings illustrate how industry leaders and firms view investment professionals on both the buy and sell sides. The survey of institutional investors collects unbiased, data-driven research from stakeholders including investment managers, buy-side firms, and corporate issuers to assess best-in-class advisory and execution services, corporate governance, and IR effectiveness. As ESG concerns at large investment firms trickle down to the CEO and CIO levels, analysts and portfolio managers will need to increase their own mid-management engagement in identifying and addressing key ESG issues.

New investment firms can enhance existing portfolio companies by providing additional financing and expertise. Expertise in procurement management, management teams that handle fixed roles and responsibilities, strategy, business growth, governance structures, cost sharing, and exit strategies all play key roles in the success of portfolio companies. When top talent is engaged in emerging industries, firms can help portfolio companies achieve revenue, earnings, and growth by providing expertise, networks, and connections.

Private equity firms have the opportunity to add value to their portfolio companies, achieve high returns, and attract new capital for reinvestment to drive growth in assets under management (AUM). TPG Capital is one of the firms pursuing this strategy and has utilized the SPAC route in recent years through exits and acquisitions. Forty-five SPACs targeting private equity portfolio companies are entering the market.

Large companies, whose shares are held by major passive asset managers and pension funds, will soon experience a fundamental shift in how investors value these businesses. The general economic and financial conditions of energy-related companies changed significantly in 2020, and top firms in particular have seen market capitalization declines that outpaced equity benchmarks. Over the past two years, oil and gas companies' market capitalizations have fallen by more than 50%, most of the decline occurring last year as investors reassessed risk and profitability expectations in the face of low oil prices, rising oversupply, and uncertainty about how effectively companies are positioning themselves in a changing market environment.

Surface-level data gathering is a poor substitute for comprehensive ESG information reported by companies. In response, companies should publish statements to share integrated reports with investors, increase mid-management engagement, and improve internal systems for measuring and reporting the ESG impact on performance data. Active managers who plan to hold shares for the long term, as well as passive managers who do the same, have an incentive to determine whether companies are addressing material ESG issues to improve financial performance.

Your balance sheet presents a snapshot of the assets your company owns and the liabilities it owes. Return on capital employed (ROCE) indicates how effectively management uses the company's resources and assets. Using balance sheet data from Doobie & Company, for example, one can calculate a leverage ratio for the company.

For illustration, dollar-cost averaging results in a lower average share price during periods when the overall market price (the purchase of an equal number of shares each month) is higher.

If investors care about returns, they may drive down share prices.

If an investor expects a 6% annual return (including dividends) before inflation and inflation is running at 2% per year, they can anticipate an 8% annual return after accounting for inflation, given the long-term returns of stocks over many decades. In a high-inflation market, lower expectations for earnings growth will place downward pressure on the share price.

The dotcom boom and bust is an excellent example of companies whose earnings fell short of investors' expectations. A company with a soaring share price may not be earning as much as it should, but investors may still hope it will become profitable in the future. There is no guarantee that the company will meet current investor expectations.

If the economy emerges from its initial recovery and growth slows, interest-rate-sensitive sectors will perform well, and stocks in sectors with the highest demand for their products and services (as a result of consolidating expansion) will yield high returns. Attractive valuations are bolstered by rising earnings expectations. A strong sales recovery, combined with measured costs and investment growth, will prompt analysts to revise earnings estimates upward according to Bloomberg consensus, favoring it over average returns.

As companies invest in the energy sector to shift away from fossil fuel business models, the return on investment in the U.S. may be lower than in Europe. Many large companies in the sector are expected to adhere to disciplined spending controls and sacrifice growth rates for higher-quality financing. The growth phase of the business cycle supports the cyclical value of energy companies as large and diversified firms become more disciplined in spending and investment.

As a result, higher inflation and interest rates could negatively affect these companies' future profitability. Stock prices tend to be volatile, and there is a significant risk of losses.

Stock market and sector returns are influenced by all phases of the business cycle. Corporate earnings, interest rates, inflation, and other factors that fluctuate as the economy expands or contracts can affect the performance of different segments of the stock market. For investors interested in an active approach to managing their equity portfolios, it can be helpful to understand how each segment of the market performs at different stages of the cycle.

Many investors use asset allocation to diversify their investments across asset classes. For example, prudent investors do not change their asset allocation solely based on the relative performance of each asset class, but may increase the portion of equities in a portfolio when the stock market is strong. Throughout the business cycle, a robust approach to investment analysis can identify key stages of the economy and offer guidance for investors as they adjust equity allocations across sectors.

Investment funds are entities that pool money from many investors and invest in stocks, bonds, and other financial instruments. Investors can diversify across different stock market sectors. For example, a stock index fund holds shares in thousands of companies.

To this end, investors should seek independent legal and financial advice before making investment decisions, including advice on tax implications. Research, analysis, and recommendations are speculative in nature, are not guaranteed, and are not intended to predict the future performance of specific Morgan Stanley Investment Management products. This is not a professional investor report. It has been provided to Morgan Stanley Investment Management Japan Co., Ltd. (AMSimja) in reference to the Discretionary Investment Management Agreement (AIMAA) and the Investment Advisory Agreement (AIIAAA).

In short, do not assume that a stock's price will rise indefinitely. For example, look for signals from investors a few weeks or even months before earnings are released.

For instance, it shows that pro forma earnings are more closely related to GAAP earnings and equity returns than corrections to analyst earnings forecasts, and that they are a better predictor of future earnings. Research likewise indicates that the earnings announcement featured in the headline or first paragraph of a company's news release has a greater impact on share prices than the pro forma earnings highlighted in the release itself. Share price movements after an earnings announcement provide substantial insight into investors' growth expectations and their perception of management's credibility.

As a result, there is no guarantee that an ESG strategy will yield favorable investment performance. Earnings before interest and taxes (EBIT or EBITA) is a measure of a company's profit that includes earnings before expenses, operating and non-operating interest costs, and earnings after tax expenses.

Investors and analysts use EPS (earnings per share) to compare the profitability of different companies. EPS shows how much a company earns per share, and a higher EPS indicates that the stock is more valuable than others in the industry. However, companies have different numbers of shares, and simply comparing earnings figures does not reveal how much money a company makes per share, so EPS is needed for a valid comparison.

If you have a growth company that earns 10 cents next year, 20 cents the following year, 40 cents the year after that, and so on, by the end of 10 years it is expected to earn 10 dollars. Investors buy growth stocks by estimating the present value of future income streams. The value of a company earning one dollar per year in ten years is the sum of the values of those future profits.

As a result, an investor nearing this financial goal may increase their bond holdings relative to equity holdings to reduce risk, or hold more bonds that may be appealing because of their lower but more stable growth potential.

Chapter 10 - Average Trading P/E Ratio of Equity and Stocks

If the fairness ratio rises, traders believe that destiny profits will be higher than the cutting-edge rate of growth, as defined by the stock. The P/E ratio will rise if earnings fall and the share price remains the same, suggesting that the organisation is not as valuable as its price implies.

The Price-earnings ratio (P/E) is a multiple or comparable relative valuation measure that looks at the historical P/E of stocks with similar values to analyze whether a stock is hyped up or undervalued at modern levels. In general, a lower P/E suggests that a stock is undervalued and performing well, while a higher P/E suggests that the stock is hyped up and traders expect its performance to improve in the destiny.

For example, a P/E of 5x means the share price of the organisation is five times its annual earnings per share. Another way to think about an organisation's P/E is to consider it as the price investors would pay for 1% of earnings per year. For instance, if a company sells at a 1.5 P/E ratio, it means investors are willing to pay $15 for every $1 of earnings.

If a share is traded at $20 per share and earns $2 in EPS (TTM) for the next 365 days, it has a P/E of 10, 20, or 2.

The P/E is a measure of the relationship between a company's share price, earnings, and newly issued shares. It is calculated by dividing the organisation's current share price by its earnings per share (EPS). If you do not know what EPS is, you can calculate it by determining the organisation's earnings, subtracting its preferred dividend from net income, and dividing by the number of outstanding shares.

Suppose the organisation has a net profit of $1 billion, pays $200 million in preferred dividends, and has 400 million shares outstanding. In addition to including the S&P 500 price per share and comparing it to the total earnings per share produced by the company, you would calculate the P/E for the US stock market. The P/E can also be compared with the sector or industry as a measure of the price-to-earnings ratio used to forecast the earnings calculation (P/E) for the next financial year.

If future profit growth is expected, the P/E should be lower than the current P/E used to calculate the value of the shares without taking profit growth into account.

The PEG ratio is calculated by dividing the P/E by the stock's expected growth rate, assessing an organisation's value based on current earnings and future growth prospects. The price-earnings ratio (P/E) used to determine a stock's value is based on subsequent earnings, takes the organisation's future income growth into consideration, and is considered more complete than the basic P/E ratio.

The PEG ratio, one of the most common financial metrics for valuing shares, is used to determine a stock's value based on an organisation's earnings growth. In other words, the price-to-earnings (P/E) ratio helps investors calculate whether a stock's price is hyped up or undervalued based on today's earnings and the organisation's expected growth rate in the future. The PEG is considered more useful than the P/E ratio because it takes the company's growth rate into account.

As a rule of thumb, stocks with a P/E of 1 are considered undervalued relative to their EPS growth rate, while shares with a P/E of 1 are considered overvalued. The P/E ratio is a large part of a value-investment strategy, which seeks companies and stocks that appear to trade below their fundamental value. For example, a high P/E can indicate whether a share price is undervalued relative to the organisation's earnings or puffed up.

When it comes to the earnings part of the calculation, there are three specific approaches to P/E that can make different statements about a stock. Although the math behind the ratio is fairly simple (price divided by earnings), there are many ways to consider the ratio of earnings and price used in the calculation.

The P/E represents a share price divided by its 12-month earnings growth value, and there are three different types of ratios based on specific earnings periods. The ratio is calculated using either the current share price or the average price over a certain time frame.

The price-earnings ratio (P/E) is a measure that helps investors evaluate a stock's trading price relative to other companies. The P/E shows not only whether an organisation's share price is overpriced or undervalued, but also how that stock is valued compared to its industry group or a benchmark like the S&P 500 Index. When analysts and investors assess an organisation's P/E, they determine what the share price represents for projected earnings per share.

It is calculated by dividing the current closing price of the stock by the last quarter's cash per share, which compares an organisation's market value to its annual free cash flow. EPS is the portion of a company's earnings attributable to outstanding common shares. An organisation's price-to-earnings (P/E) ratio compares its current share price to its earnings per share (EPS), which is calculated based on historical data, next P/E, and future P/E estimates. The P/E can be calculated simply by dividing the share price by its earnings or investment return, which you can find by dividing the organisation's earnings by the share price at the current level.

Historically, stocks have averaged a P/E ratio between 15 and 20. If you examine a large database of companies, you will find that most shares have traded within this range.

The stock market as a whole, as measured by the S&P 500, has had an average P/E ratio of 15.54 throughout its history. Its lowest recorded P/E ratio was 5.31 in 1917, and its highest record was 123.73 in May 2009.

Chapter 11 - The Long Term ROE Trends and Stock Performance

ROE is calculated by dividing a corporation's net income by its equity. The formula for calculating ROE for a company is its net income divided by shareholders' equity, as noted above. However, ROE can also be calculated by simply dividing a company's net income by its shareholders' equity, which measures how well management uses investors' money to generate income.

While ROE examines how much profit a company generates relative to its shareholders' shares, ROIC (Return on Invested Capital) goes further. ROE looks at how effectively a company uses equity, while ROIC is designed to determine how efficiently a company uses its available capital to make money. ROI is calculated using net income less dividends in the numerator and the sum of the company's debt and equity in the denominator.

Return on equity (ROE) is a measure of financial performance that indicates how profitable a company is. It measures a company's financial performance and shows the relationship between the company's profits and investor returns. ROE is the financial metric that tells you how much net income a company can generate for every dollar of capital invested.

On average, since shareholders' equity equals assets minus liabilities, ROE measures the return generated by a company's net assets. If shareholders' equity equals the company's assets minus its debt, ROE is considered a return on net assets.

Return on equity (ROE) is a useful measure of a company's return on capital within a particular industry. Understanding what ROE means and how to evaluate companies with it can help you develop smart investment strategies. ROE is one of the most important financial metrics for equity investors seeking the best value in a company.

As a rule, net income to equity should be a positive number to illustrate ROE. A high ROE signals that the company is using its equity to generate returns. For example, if 1% of a company's share capital generates 10% of net income, shareholders get a return of 10% on their investment.

Return on equity (ROE) is a measure of a company's annual return on net income or on earnings from key positions that are not included in the income statement or the three core financial statements. To calculate ROE, analysts divide the company's net income by the average shareholder equity.

A high ROE means that the company has effectively generated profits. A sustained increase in ROE over time means that the company is skilled at delivering what shareholders value as the financial benefit of owning its shares. If the ROE is positive (return on investment) and the ROI is negative, the company may be using borrowed money to generate profits in order to survive.

On a corporate basis, a negative ROE can be caused by factors such as restructuring, which negatively impacts net income and leads to a net loss. In addition to changes in net income, ROE also affects the level of corporate borrowing. If a company has negative returns or negative equity, it can lead to a higher ROE.

Simply put, ROE allows investors to see whether they are getting a good return on their money in a company and how the company uses its equity. To satisfy investors, a company must be able to generate high ROE and be considered a low-risk investment. ROE also provides insights into how corporate governance manages finance and equity to grow the business.

Suppose a company generates a profit of R 100,000 per 1,000 shares of shareholders, each worth R 50. The company has an ROE of 15% and returns 30% of its net income to shareholders as dividends, meaning it retains 70% of its net income. In the same sector, ROE levels can vary depending on whether a company decides to pay dividends and on how it handles its earnings.

A decline in ROE indicates that the company has become less efficient at generating profits and increasing shareholder value. Share buybacks and asset write-downs can cause ROE to rise even when corporate profits fall. The average ROE over time, such as five or ten years, provides insight into a company's growth history.

Venison is harvested from wild salmon (keta), also called chum salmon, which can be a bargain at $7 an ounce. Once the fish is harvested, large quantities of it are processed into roe.

It seems a shame to throw it away, knowing that roe, like other fish, is delicious. Sea urchin roe was prized as a permissible delicacy during the long Lent season. Roe has been commended by committees over the years for playing a prominent role in selecting applications.

ROE is the ratio of a listed corporation's net income to its equity, which represents the value of the company's assets minus its liabilities. Since a company's equity is equal to its assets minus its debt, ROE is considered a return on net assets. On average, shareholders' equity measures the return generated by a company's net assets.

Return on equity (ROE) is a financial indicator that shows how much profit a listed company generates relative to its net assets. It measures how well a company generates income for its owners. By comparing a company's net income to its shareholders' equity, ROE helps investors understand how the company uses their money to generate profits.

As ROE examines how much income a company generates relative to return on invested capital (ROIC), it takes this analysis a few steps further. ROE examines how effectively a company uses its available capital to earn money.

If the company has preferred super preference shares, the ratio indicator becomes the net result plus the annual preference dividend. Shareholders are interested in the ratio of operating income to operating assets as a measure of how efficiently management uses those assets, but they are also interested in the return the company earns per dollar of equity. Results show that when 1% of a company's share capital generates 10% of net income, shareholders get a 10% return on their investment.

The long-term equity ratio shows the relationship between a company's debt and equity financing. This ratio provides an indication of a company's long-term liquidity and the extent to which it uses long-term debt to support the business. Return on Assets (ROA) is a measure of how well a company performs relative to the profit (or net income) it generates from its capital investment in assets.

The terms shares or equity are used interchangeably, but equity typically represents a fraction of a company's ownership. The stock market is where investors can buy and sell such ownership. Financial assets arise from contractual agreements or future cash flows held by equity instruments or corporations. The secondary purpose of the market is to give investors who buy shares the opportunity to share in the profits of listed companies.

This approach is based on the assumption that the price of a share corresponds to the current value of its future dividends, discounted by the company's equity costs. For example, if an investor buys shares at $10 each and the price rises to $15, he would earn a 50% return on his investment by selling them.

The expected return on a company's shares to shareholders is the opportunity cost of the equity funds used by the company. If a company theoretically generates the cost of equity (equity financed partly by its investments), its share price could fall. However, if the company does not generate at least the cost of equity, its return on capital might still achieve the expected return of other securities with similar risk levels in the financial market.

Return on Assets (ROA), which measures a company's net income divided by its total assets, is similar to ROE, and the formulas are alike except that ROE factors debt into whether a company is profitable. While ROE may be positive (return on investment), ROI can be negative if a company uses borrowed money to survive. Return on Capital Employed (ROCE) is also used to analyze a company.

If a company has several years of losses that reduce shareholders' equity but then enjoys profitable years, the asset denominator can shift. In addition to changes in net income, ROE also affects how much a company might borrow.

Negative ROE for companies with net losses or negative equity should not be used to analyze them, but companies that have positive ROE can be assessed in comparison. Most investors avoid investing in companies that do not provide positive returns, though they might overlook a negative return in a single difficult year if they believe the company is well positioned for long-term growth.

Return on average capital stock is an important measure of a company's profitability from the shareholders' point of view, and the relationship between it and ROE is referred to as return on average capital stock or return on equity (ROE). To calculate ROE, analysts divide a company's net income by the average equity of its shareholders. The net income and shareholders' equity from the company's balance sheet represent what is left to shareholders after liquidation and repayment of debts.

If you are considering investing in the stock market, you can examine the average returns of large listed companies to understand what a good return might look like. Calculating an individual company's ROE can provide insights into its comparative value, but average ROEs vary by industry. It is wise to add context to a company's ROE by calculating the ROE of its competitors within the same sector.

There are countless metrics and measurements that investors use to assess a company's overall financial health and to calculate the intrinsic value of its shares. The most common analysis tool is the profitability ratio, a cross-sectional analysis that compares several companies' indicators in the same industry.

This method is based on the assumption that the price of a share should match the present value of its future dividends per share, subtracting the company's equity cost. If a corporate investment yielding 3.85% is turned into a dividend per share buyback opportunity yielding 7.33%, the market, due to its apparent irrationality, will discount the company's capital investment and increase its implied return.

This allows the general present value formula to convert into a simple equity equation that produces a consistent rate of growth below the company's cost of equity. The problem with using a dividend growth model to estimate the cost of equity is that the index g should come from a stable equity cost ratio, not just the expected growth rate that investors often use when evaluating stocks.

Because there is a relationship between a company's profits and investors' returns, ROE is an important metric to consider. Despite the drawbacks of using ROE, the main conclusion is that ROE should be valued when evaluating a share, excluding intangible assets such as intellectual property and brand recognition from the calculation. Return on Equity (ROE) helps investors distinguish between a company that generates profits and one that consumes them.

ROI is calculated by dividing a company's net income by its shareholders' equity to measure how effectively it generates profits. By measuring a company's returns from assets, ROE provides a gauge of profitable performance. The traditional way of calculating a company's return on capital is to divide net income attributable to common shareholders (from the income statement) by the equity of common shareholders (from the balance sheet).

From the shareholders' perspective, the most important measure of a company's profitability is the ratio between the average return on equity (the so-called return on equity) and the average return on equity (ROE). While shareholders are interested in the ratio of operating income to operating assets as a measure of management's efficient use of assets, they are also interested in the return that a company earns per dollar of equity. Market-to-book multiples have been shown to be driven by ROE (r = g/r), where g is the growth rate, r is the cost of equity, and ROE is the company's return on equity of its average common equity.

To measure the value of a company's shares, multiply the current share price by the outstanding diluted shares. If the company has preferred outstanding stock, the return on each dollar of shareholder equity earned by the company is net income plus the annual preferred dividend.

Enterprise value represents the total worth of a company at a given time, factoring in its actual share prices and balance sheet costs. In theory, if a company generates the cost of equity (equity financed partly by its investment), its share price could fall. However, if it does not generate at least the cost of equity, then its return for fund shareholders will align with the expected return of all other securities with a similar level of risk in the financial market.

This ratio is useful for evaluating companies that are unprofitable or going through challenging times. Simply put, ROE reveals how effectively management uses investors' capital.

Investors looking for profitable equity investments should also review other important indicators, such as Return on Invested Capital (ROIC), Earnings Per Share (EPS), and Return on Assets Total (ROTA). This study provides comprehensive panel regression results to explain Return on Assets (ROA) versus Return on Equity (ROE). Unlike the inflated ROE figures calculated using a conventional nominal approach, this method produces ROIE numbers that are more meaningful and consistent with other data about companies: their actual returns and their average cost of equity.

Research shows that projected earnings per share (E/P) and ROE are statistically significant in explaining part of the Shanghai Stock Exchange (SSE) return in a flat multifactor model, as Clubb and Naffi (2007) suggest. These findings support the conclusion that aggregated forecast variables (FRM) and the inclusion of the forecast earnings yield (FEP) and forecast return on equity (FROE) explain some of the fluctuations in SSE market returns.

The authors recommend that future researchers conduct relevant studies on the inclusion of the BM ratio as a benchmark for comparative analysis of the E/P ratio to see if it has a significant impact on fluctuations in Chinese equity returns.

In financial markets, equity valuation is a method of calculating the theoretical value of companies and their shares. The market-to-book ratio helps a company determine whether the value of its assets corresponds to the market value of its shares.

The market-to-book ratio, also called the price-to-book ratio, is a financial metric used to measure a company's current market value relative to its book value. The market-to-book multiple is driven by return on equity, which is also the main driver of the price-to-earnings (P/E) multiple. The price-to-earnings ratio is the relationship between a company's share price and its earnings per share. The ratio of equity to long-term solvency indicates the relationship between a company's debt and equity financing.

Because there is a relationship between a company's profits and investors' returns, ROE is the most valuable metric to observe. Although a higher ROE often implies a higher share price, predicting a company's share price based on ROE alone depends on many factors besides ROE itself. Despite the limitations in using ROE, the main takeaway is that return on equity (ROE) should only be used when valuing a share if the company's intangible assets, such as intellectual property and brand recognition, are excluded from the calculation.

Return on equity (ROE) is a ratio that measures the return a company's common shareholders earn on their investment. Unlike certain financial metrics, ROE reflects how well a company is performing by indicating how much revenue it can generate from shareholders' capital. By comparing a listed company's net income to its shareholders' equity, you can see how the company uses investors' money to generate profits.

ROE is the ratio of a listed company's net income to its equity, which represents the value of its assets minus its liabilities. Shareholder equity is also called shareholders' equity, because it is the amount contributed by those who hold its shares. When a company buys back shares or increases dividends, average equity can fall, leading to a higher return.

As a measure of profitability, a company's equity ratio rises when the carrying amount of equity grows. A higher ratio shows that the company generates more profit for every dollar of equity available to shareholders. ROE is a useful indicator of financial success because it demonstrates that the company is making a profit without injecting new equity.

ROE is a ratio of net income to average equity, and many financial factors can influence it, such as changes in net income and fluctuations in equity. Inconsistent earnings, excessive debt, and negative net income all affect return on equity for common shareholders. Investors combine ROE with other financial indicators to analyze and compare companies across industries.

Return on Equity (ROE) compares the accounting profits attributable to equity holders and measures the value shareholders receive for the price they pay per share. It is beneficial to compare a company's return on capital with its cost of equity, which is the return shareholders require for investing in the company. Return on equity can be distorted by share buybacks. Dividends, share buybacks, and repurchases are all ways shareholders earn returns from listed companies.

Return on equity (ROE) helps investors distinguish between companies that generate profits and those that burn money. It helps them decide whether a company is a lean, profitable machine or an inefficient operator. Total return drives overall returns and determines how much investors pay out in shares later, based on the company's dividend policy.

Return on capital employed (ROE) measures management's capacity to generate revenue from the equity available to it. Simply put, ROE lets investors see whether they are getting a good return on their money by measuring how well the company uses its equity. By measuring the returns a company generates from assets, Return on Equity (ROE) provides a gauge of profitable performance.

Return on Equity (ROE) is calculated by dividing a company's net income by its shareholder equity to measure how efficiently the company generates profits. It is a financial ratio that shows how much profit a public company earns compared to its net assets. ROE is measured by the company's annual return (net income), which is a key item not explicitly listed on the income statement but referenced among the three core financial statements.

Return on assets measures a company's net income divided by its total assets. It is similar to ROE, but ROE factors in debt to see if the company makes a profit. At the same time, ROE from the income statement can be a better gauge of financial performance than profitability measured only as return on sales. To measure profitability, a company's equity is calculated by dividing the company's earnings by its average equity for each accounting period.

An ROE equals the net income margin multiplied by net assets, multiplied by the accounting leverage of total assets divided by total liabilities. For a company, ROE should be 1 if that means 1 average share generates a net income of 1. If a company succeeds in raising its earnings after interest by 12%, then its Return on Capital Employed (ROCE) and its profitability ratio measure how effectively it uses its capital to produce profits.

Return on equity (ROE) is a measure of a company's ability to generate profits based on shareholders' portion of its equity. Over time, the interest coverage ratio (operating income divided by net interest expense for the last four quarters) measures the safety margin for lenders and ensures the company's earnings are sufficient to cover annual interest payments. If interest payments exceed the return on the company's balance sheet total, which measures profits before interest and taxes relative to its net assets, the negative leverage effect is removed.

Dividing net income by shareholders shows that a second company might have a higher ROE due to financial indebtedness. One aspect of the DuPont equation is profit margins, which grow when revenue adds more cash to net income, resulting in an overall higher return on equity. If rising prices and rising profits are the end result, the company achieves a higher return on its shares by raising prices 13% and overall profits by 65%.

Chapter 12 - Technology Sector and Correlations Studies

The technology sector is large and includes, to name a few, machine manufacturers, software developers, wireless companies, streaming services, semiconductor companies, and cloud computing providers. It is anchored by semiconductors, computer hardware, and communication devices. In addition, software companies are expanding the sector by adding anything code-based.

There are many valuable companies in the world of technology. The technology sector consists of companies selling goods and services in electronics, software, computers, artificial intelligence, and other related IT (Information Technology) industries. The IT sector includes organizations that manufacture software, hardware, and semiconductor equipment, as well as companies that provide Internet-related services.

The technology sector encompasses companies involved in the manufacture of electronics, the development of software and computer products, and information technology-related services. In business, there are numerous products and services related to information technology, including computers, software, electronics, semiconductors, the Internet, telecommunications equipment, and e-commerce. The three fundamental industry groups within the information technology (IT) sector are software and services, technological hardware and equipment, and semiconductors and semiconductor equipment.

It consists of multiple layers of physical equipment, whether software or hardware, including hardware, virtualization, control systems, automation tools, operating systems, and other software and applications used to perform vital functions. System software includes computer programs that manage basic computing capabilities. A computer operating system or software-based command set refers to the complex command set of a computer.

Hardware includes components such as microprocessors, hard drives, memory chips, and graphics cards. Individual hardware parts added to primary computer devices—such as monitors, modems, printers, and keyboards—are known as peripherals.

This process translates the layout of hardware components into software components. One might imagine the hardware of a vehicle as software and the driver as the fuel the vehicle needs to run. Modules refer to technologies that encompass both hardware and software in a computer and require both to operate within the system.

The automation of manufacturing systems is a method that involves using computers to communicate work commands, automate the handling and processing of machines, control processes numerically, operate robots, and plan material requirements for the production of workpieces.

In a business context, the Information Technology Association of America defines information technology as the study, design, development, application, implementation, support, and management of computerized information systems.

Information technology (IT) is the use of computers, storage media, networks, and other physical devices and infrastructures in the process of creating, processing, storing, securing, and transferring any form of digital data. It covers the basic principles of computer-aided information systems, including computer hardware, operating systems (OSs), programs, software, and data processes that produce useful information. An information technology system (IT system, information system, or communication system, so to speak) is a computer-based system made up of hardware, software, and peripherals, operated by a limited group of IT users.

Technology is the knowledge and application of specific techniques and skills in developing products and services that meet particular needs. Knowledge of information technology is required to identify hardware and software components that can be used to improve certain business processes.

This document is intended to serve as a glossary of terminology for software development, computer systems, the FDA, and regulated industries. Computer technology is the study of computers, including their theoretical and algorithmic foundations, hardware, software, and their use for data processing. It applies the concepts of mathematics, technology, and logic to a wide range of functions, including algorithm design, software and hardware development, and artificial intelligence.

Security and information security involve designing computer systems and software to protect the integrity and safety of data, as well as the privacy of individuals identified by that data.

Technology, hardware, memory, and peripherals are the groups that manufacture cell phones, PCs, servers, electronics, computer products, and peripherals. As you can see, the tech industry appears to be all-encompassing, but it can be broken into subsectors such as semiconductors, networks, software, hardware, and the Internet to help gauge its scale.

Some companies sell hardware and technology equipment to various enterprises that do not manufacture or sell equipment directly to customers, including those that distribute communication systems and computer semiconductors. Examples of such companies include Apple, HP, Dell, Motorola, Cisco Systems, SanDisk, and Western Digital.

It is also the market where large software companies such as Novell, which provides network software, and Oracle, which offers database software, conduct most of their business.

With the growth of network computers in most institutions, the role of minicomputers has expanded. PCs, along with laptops and notebooks with monitors, keyboards, and CPUs, have become practical and flexible business tools that can function as part of an organizational network. High-performance computing is not only used on PCs but also on minicomputers.

Businesses, on the other hand, rely on technology to develop corporate software, streamline their systems, host their databases, and maintain information that affects their operations, employees, and customers.

Video streaming companies that provide easy access to high-quality content, along with the cloud computing providers that power them, offer industry-leading services. These companies dominate their industries, and their stocks have delivered impressive returns in recent years. However, there are many competing platforms and standards, and numerous different providers (device manufacturers, software companies, and network operators) all want a share of the market.

Below is a list of more than two hundred ETFs, index funds, and mutual funds tracking the IT sector and specific industries such as semiconductors, the Internet, and software. Electronic payment systems are software platforms used to make payments over computer networks, while smart cards are systems used to purchase goods from companies, and chip card hardware is a hybrid device.

IBM traders use futures to speculate on the price movements of IBM stock in order to make a profit. Traders open a long (buy) position if they believe IBM's share price will rise, and a short (sell) position if they believe IBM's price will fall.

Traders speculate on the movement of IBM's share price by owning IBM stock. Long-term investors purchase traditional IBM shares for long-term stability. Investors keep trading IBM over the long term because shares are bought and sold every day.

The majority of investors want to buy and sell IBM shares in order to profit from price fluctuations. The situation is different if you cannot buy IBM stock due to the free cash flow of 10% and a dividend yield of 5%. Investors are considering purchasing IBM shares to try to make gains when the price rises.

In the short term, IBM still appears more attractive to traders and investors. Before the report, analysts had forecast revenue of 75.2 billion dollars and earnings per share (EPS) of 7.92 dollars for 2021. Analysts took a more negative view of the business after the report, slightly lowering their EPS forecasts for the year ahead. The average price target remained steady at around 149 dollars, but analysts voted for lower earnings forecasts, which are unlikely to result in a lower share price anytime soon.

A total of 15 analysts provided 12-month forecasts for International Business Machines Corp. IBM's median price target was 14,000 dollars, with the highest estimate at 16,500 dollars and the lowest estimate at 11,500 dollars. Analysts said IBM's stock could reach 110 to 100 dollars per share in the next few months.

In the third quarter, IBM reduced its full-year earnings estimates, taking into account, among other factors, the impact of its acquisition of Red Hat. IBM shares dropped despite gains, and investors do not expect the situation to improve anytime soon.

Since 2010, IBM's revenue has been around 100 billion dollars, but it has declined every year since then, with the average dropping 3% to 73.6 billion dollars by 2020, according to Macrotrends. An IBM spokesman declined to comment on IBM's earnings when the share price fell. Analysts have questioned

IBM's forecast of mid-single-digit revenue growth after the company spun off one of its largest divisions in an earnings spin-off released on Thursday.

In the past eleven quarters, only one showed year-over-year revenue growth. Two of the company's five segments reported year-over-year revenue declines in the previous quarter. According to Refinitiv, IBM's annualized revenue slipped 6% to 207.7 billion dollars, or 400 million dollars below analysts' estimates overall.

Ellis's calculations and adjustments suggest that, once accounting for the billions in restructuring costs IBM is trying to eliminate, the company shows the same lack of earnings growth indicated by its other figures.

IBM's relative strength has remained consistent with a sideways trend so far this year. The company's stock has risen slightly, but its relative strength aligns with the overall sideways movement for the year.

Whether it concerns enterprise operations or economic health in general, IBM's success depends on how comprehensive and integrated your fundamental analysis is when trading IBM shares. Here are six key elements that IBM traders and investors should examine. This information must be closely monitored by traders, as it will affect IBM's forecast share price in the short and medium term.

Nevertheless, the company's long-term earnings performance will be much more important next year. Special attention should be paid to how well IBM plans to diversify its product range, as this remains one of the company's primary risk factors.

With a dividend yield of up to 5.28% and a P/E ratio of just 14%, IBM has introduced some interesting spin-offs that have prompted the market to reconsider its view of the company's stock. Investors seem to have more reason to pay close attention to IBM's upcoming earnings report. Analysts are not entirely positive about IBM's strategy, and there are reasons to be pessimistic about the company's future.

The IBD Big Cap 20 Index offers a selection of large-cap stocks. If you want to invest in these stocks, this is the place to look. IBM, in its current form, including its 2021 stock evaluation and dividend review, may be considered today.

If you are looking for the best stocks to buy or watch, check out the IBM Stock List and other IBM research sources. Read our final Big Picture column daily to ensure growth investors have the green light.

Some prominent investment firms argue that the combination of overall market and sector movements, along with a company's individual performance, determines the majority of equity price movements. Fundamental factors driving share prices are based on a company's revenue and profitability from producing and selling goods and services. Technical factors relate to share price trends, market history in terms of chart patterns and dynamics, and the behavioral factors of traders and investors.

Holders of common stock record profit before earnings per share (EPS) as their return on investment. If you invest in the stock market, there are fewer shares in circulation, which supports earnings per share. IBM's stock dividend has risen alongside its earnings per share.

Most of IBM's business units have struggled to achieve significant growth in recent years. A major shift in enterprise operations helps explain the increase in revenue and earnings struggles. From strong customers to weaker ones, IBM reduced its sales by lowering Salesforce's commissions.

Companies and stocks tend to follow the market closely, along with their sector and industry peers. Prominent investment firms argue that the combination of overall market and sector movements, plus a company's individual performance, determines the majority of equity price movements. Fundamental factors driving share prices are based on the company's earnings and profitability from producing and selling goods and services. Technical factors relate to share prices, the market's history in terms of chart patterns and dynamics, and the behavioral elements of traders and investors.

Major takeaways: share prices are driven by a variety of factors, and prices at any given time are determined by supply and demand in the market. Fundamental factors that drive stock prices are based on a company's earnings and profitability from producing and selling goods and services. Technical factors relate to share prices, the market's history in terms of chart patterns and dynamics, and the behavioral aspects of investors and traders.

The price of a stock on any given day is shaped by the whims of "Mr. Market" (Warren Buffett's metaphor) and the broader stock market's fluctuations. Investors need to consider price patterns and form opinions about market trends in a short span of time, especially when stock prices are volatile. By examining long-term price patterns, you can see clearly defined trends. If you want to understand stock market movements, you must also understand the market's language.

Over the long term, share prices are governed by a handful of fundamental factors, such as earnings growth and valuation shifts. Trading is conducted on an equity basis, and share prices generally move in tandem with news, political events, economic reports, and other factors. The first step in understanding and evaluating the causes of stock market trends is to identify the elements that influence Dalal Street's buzz: a change in interest rates triggers a flurry of trading actions in the stock market.

While technical analysis can influence stock prices in the short term, the value of the stock ultimately depends on a company's long-term profitability. Politics is constant, but the market ultimately measures just one factor: where investors believe corporate profits are headed in the future.

Political conditions, negotiations between countries and corporations, product breakthroughs, mergers and acquisitions, and other unforeseen events can affect stocks and the stock market. If you can imagine how the cycle of supply and demand repeats for millions of traders in equities around the world each trading day, you can grasp the mechanisms that drive daily fluctuations in stock prices. There is evidence that the market is not always fully efficient in how readily available information is processed and reflected in market prices.

Think of the stock market as a massive auction, with traders bidding for one share or another while offering to sell their own. As investors buy and sell stocks, their exchanges track supply and demand for listed equities. This helps determine the price of securities and the level at which market participants (investors and traders) are willing to buy or sell.

Investors buy and sell shares in the hope of profiting from price movements. This is a simple explanation of how people make money in the stock market, but it does not clarify why ups and downs occur. Investors aim to buy a stock and sell it at a profit when its share price rises.

Active stock selection is based on the false belief that the market is pricing shares incorrectly. When stock prices are decoupled from fundamentals, it reinforces public perception that markets are manipulated by a small group of insiders on whom a large group of determined investors cannot rely. This has long-term implications for what happens to AMC, GameStop, and other headline-grabbing stocks.

All else being equal, a higher interest rate reduces the present value of a company's future cash flows, depressing its share price. Conversely, a lower interest rate makes future cash flows more valuable, resulting in higher share prices.

Economic growth, for example, contributes to earnings growth. A growing economy can lead to higher inflation and higher interest rates, which can be beneficial for stocks but only to a limited extent. This can result in declining stock markets. Inflation is an increase in the cost of goods and services over a certain period. Large fluctuations are caused by market volatility, during which share prices rise and fall.

While the Nasdaq Composite has gained 856% and the S&P 500 has gained 195% since 1999, more stocks have lost value than gained as investors sold shares in slow-growing companies and invested in Internet-based firms. Most technology shares during the dotcom bubble had a beta higher than 1, meaning their decline during recessions exceeded twice the market average.

The enthusiasm for buying Internet-based shares was so overwhelming that many so-called "dotcoms" were established, because they operated in a fast-growing sector and needed financing. The stock market crash that struck the NASDAQ exchange was a shock event that led to a massive sell-off in shares, as demand dropped and restrictions on venture capital financing accelerated the decline. Compared with how similar companies are valued through intrinsic valuation (which considers a company's inherent worth), it caused market panic. The large sell-off of dotcom companies and shares in 2002 led to a dramatic fall in value, with investors' losses estimated at 5 trillion dollars.

There has been no real positive news for IBM's shares since the third-quarter earnings statement. Shareholders have reason to be cautious: IBM has a large product portfolio, and when the returns from that portfolio are insufficient, it is natural for investors to want to see the results and hear about opportunities. Analysts update their forecasts after each earnings report to get a broader perspective, and we can judge them based on how their views on IBM have changed and what new concerns need to be addressed.

Cloud revenue led the pack with an annual figure of 12.7 billion dollars, placing IBM at the top of the heap. In the first quarter, its cloud and cognitive software business, which includes Red Hat, reached 54.4 billion dollars, up 4% from analysts' estimate of 53 billion dollars in revenue.

On April 20, when IBM announced its first quarterly revenue growth since the second quarter of 2018, the gap led to a handle buyout of 137.17 dollars. Shares fell more than 1% in premarket trading as the company missed Wall Street's revenue estimates. When IBM released its results, the stock was more than 16% above the top 100 after the company reported quarterly earnings.

In the quarter, IBM earned 35.4 billion dollars, or 2.31 dollars per share, compared with 31.99 billion dollars, or 1.99 dollars per share, in the same period in 2005. On a continuing basis, the company earned 22.6 dollars per share, including a tax benefit of 6 cents per share. Without the tax benefit, IBM would have earned 21.0 dollars per share, beating analysts' estimates from Thomson Financial by one cent.

In the last eleven quarters, only one recorded an increase in earnings compared to the same period the previous year. Analysts estimate EPS at 3.34 times, which is less than the 4.5 times expected at the start of the year.

Big Blue (IBM) got things rolling early, opening up by 4%. Shares rose 2% in premarket trading before retreating. Earlier this year, IBM's stock rose 33%, signaling to investors that the Red Hat deal was far from over.

Although it is unwise to focus on a single price target, investors should examine the range of estimates to see if there is a difference of opinion on the company's valuation. Of the 28 analysts from firms tracked by S&P Global Market Intelligence, the stock received a "strong buy" rating from some, a "buy" rating from others, and a "hold" rating from nine.

Over the years, investor enthusiasm for IBM shares has waned because the company's financial products have matured and lost some of their popularity as technology stocks. Many consider its legacy business of managing infrastructure services to be a drag that could be offset by revenue from its growing high-margin cloud business. With a renewed focus on the cloud, investors could assign the new company a price-to-earnings ratio closer to that of a high-growth tech stock. In that scenario, the share price could rise after the transaction. Looking beyond the short-term perspective, IBM seems suitable for traders and investors for a while yet.

Given the importance of Friday's Investor Day, the options on International Business Machines (IBM) reflect a 2% bounce, with traders expecting the company to report on the financial impact of its recent Red Hat acquisition. IBM stock options are priced as if there is a 99-pound shortfall, yet this is a crucial event that could redefine investors' views of the management team, corporate strategy, earnings outlook, and stock valuation. Because IBM shares are part of the Dow Jones Industrial Average, which has risen 5% since earnings, the options market appears disconnected from the fact that these developments are more significant than earnings reports.

Technical analysis of the IBM share price is a key factor in determining its investment value. The IBD Stock Checkup Tool indicates that IBM has an overall score of 60 out of a possible 99 points.

IBM has a reasonable P/E ratio of 15.93 and offers a dividend of 4.71%. Unlike Cisco, IBM's early success came in an extremely high-growth market, and the stock provides shareholders with a solid 3.5% dividend yield. By rewarding long-term investors over time, IBM is ahead of Cisco in its transformation, giving it the edge in this comparison.

If IBM demonstrates sufficiently strong cloud growth in the coming years to expand the price-to-earnings ratio investors are willing to pay, that could be significant. Analysts are also ramping up promotional efforts for the iPhone maker, arguing that its recent underperformance offers investors a chance to acquire one of the best Dow Jones stocks at a more favorable price.

Of the 27 analysts covering the stock tracked by S&P Global Market Intelligence, 16 rate UNH as a strong buy, six say sell, three recommend holding, and one calls it a sell. Major investors believe the stock has reached a tipping point, with hedge fund Cavalry Management Group—which has more than 230 billion dollars in assets under management—establishing large positions in the company while the Street remains on the sidelines. The ongoing Chinese consumer backlash against Western brands has discouraged some investors, according to Stifel analyst Jim Duffy, who remains a buyer.

On December 5, the value of global equities surpassed 100 dollars for the first time ever. It is no surprise that investors are seizing the opportunity to take profits. The low valuation is largely due to declining revenue in many of the company's legacy businesses, and investors often show less interest in stocks without strong growth figures.

Companies and stocks tend to follow the market closely, along with their sector and industry peers. Prominent investment firms argue that a combination of overall market and sector movements accounts for most price fluctuations, rather than just the performance of an individual company.

Key takeaways: share prices are influenced by a variety of factors, and prices at any given time are determined by supply and demand in the market. Fundamental drivers of stock prices include a company's earnings and profitability from producing and selling goods and services. Technical factors relate to share prices, the market's history in terms of chart patterns and dynamics, and the behavioral elements of traders and investors.

The price of a stock on any given day is shaped by the whims of the market. Investors must consider price patterns and form opinions about market trends quickly, especially when stock prices are volatile. By examining long-term price patterns, you can see clearly defined trends. Understanding stock market movements also requires familiarity with the market's language.

Over the long term, share prices are governed by a few fundamental factors, including earnings growth and valuation changes. Trading is carried out on an equity basis, and share prices as a whole move in parallel with news, political events, economic reports, and other factors. The first step in understanding and evaluating the causes of stock market trends is to look at some of the elements that drive the market's daily fluctuations, such as changes in interest rates that often spark a wave of trading activity.

While technical analysis can affect stock prices in the short term, the fundamental value of a stock ultimately depends on a company's longer-term profitability. Politics is relatively constant, but the market focuses on anticipating future corporate earnings.

Political conditions, negotiations between countries and corporations, product breakthroughs, mergers and acquisitions, and other unexpected events can all influence stocks and the stock market. If you can envision how supply and demand cycles repeat for millions of stock traders worldwide every day, you can understand the underlying mechanisms behind daily price fluctuations. There is evidence that the market is not always fully efficient in how rapidly information is absorbed and reflected in price movements.

Think of the stock market as a massive auction, with traders competing to buy or sell shares. As traders make transactions, they track supply and demand for shares, influencing price levels and determining how willing participants are to buy or sell.

Investors buy a stock expecting to earn a profit from an increase in its share price. Active stock selection arises from the mistaken assumption that the market is pricing stocks incorrectly. When stock prices deviate from fundamental values, it strengthens the common perception that a small group of insiders manipulates the markets at the expense of a larger group of investors.

When all else is equal, a higher interest rate reduces the present value of a company's future cash flows, thereby lowering its share price. Conversely, a lower interest rate makes future cash flows more valuable, boosting share prices.

Economic growth promotes earnings expansion, but it can also trigger a rise in inflation and interest rates, which may help or harm stocks depending on how extensive the increase is. Such conditions can lead to a drop in the stock markets if the impact is too significant.

During the dotcom bubble, most tech stocks had betas above 1, making their declines during recessions more than double the market's average drop. Investors moved capital away from slow-growing companies to Internet-based startups, fueling rampant speculation.

Excessive enthusiasm for Internet-focused firms led to countless dotcom companies seeking financing to operate in a rapidly growing segment. When the NASDAQ crashed, a large sell-off ensued as demand plummeted, and venture capital restrictions magnified the decline. Intrinsic valuation, which attempts to determine a company's true worth, revealed market panic, resulting in the massive unwinding of dotcom shares in 2002 and an estimated 5 trillion dollars in investor losses.

Microsoft's potential to develop its own chip business suggests a bleak outlook for established microchip manufacturers that rely on external revenue streams. As Financial Mail notes, now might be an opportune time to invest in tech stocks. For newcomers, a brief guide to stock investing can be helpful.

Intel's growth is largely driven by its data center divisions, while Qualcomm's chip sales remain the company's main revenue engine. As the computing industry shifts from PC-centric to data-centric models, Intel faces strong competition and operational challenges.

Hedge funds gravitate toward companies gaining market share, and analysts frequently maintain a positive outlook on stocks with upward momentum. Consensus opinions often reflect these bullish perspectives, shaping investor sentiment.

Market research indicates that computer shipments increased by 14.6% to 813 million units in the third quarter, surpassing previous projections. This represents a jump from 2.7% growth in 2019 and 11.2% growth in the second quarter. Overall group revenue reached 34.7 billion dollars, exceeding the 34.37 billion forecast.

Analysts remain divided on whether stocks will experience a solid rebound or face an uncertain future. Some see the potential for continued outperformance in the coming years, while others view the current momentum as excessive.

Since 1999, the Nasdaq Composite has surged 856% and the S&P 500 has gained 195%, but many individual stocks lost value as investors left slow-growth companies in favor of Internet stocks. Meanwhile, Microsoft has delivered steady returns, partly due to its robust business model and sound fundamentals.

Tax-related selling can also prompt short-term dips in stocks, especially around key deadlines. Capital gains taxes from the previous year can lead some investors to liquidate positions, adding to the market's volatility.

The dotcom bubble originated from widespread speculation in Internet-based companies in the late 1990s. Firms like MicroStrategy rose to astonishing levels but eventually fell victim to market corrections. Despite the overall resilience of technology, the mania led to a significant crash for many unsustainable business models.

Investor Day announcements, M&A activity, and new product launches can all cause dramatic stock reactions. It is not uncommon for share prices to swing by several percentage points in response to these developments. Notably, IBM's acquisition of Red Hat remains a central topic in shareholder discussions.

Cloud revenue, which reached 12.7 billion dollars, continues to boost IBM's profile, with first-quarter results reinforcing the company's shift toward high-margin businesses. Analysts are closely watching how Red Hat's integration will further enhance IBM's performance.

IBM reported 35.4 billion dollars in quarterly revenue, an increase from 31.99 billion dollars a year earlier. On a pro forma basis, the company posted

22.6 dollars per share, which included a minor tax benefit. Excluding that benefit, IBM still slightly exceeded market forecasts, indicating continued investor confidence in its strategy.

Shares opened the day 4% higher before retracing their gains. Although up 33% for the year, the stock's performance suggests that investors are still assessing the impact of the Red Hat acquisition. Experts caution that profitability concerns and integration challenges might temper further upward momentum.

Forecasts of future valuations should always be approached with caution. Many analysts look at a range of price targets from various research firms, allowing investors to see how differing opinions shape market consensus. Meanwhile, IBM's mid-single-digit growth guidance remains under examination.

IBM's P/E ratio hovers around 15.93, accompanied by a dividend yield of approximately 4.71%. Together with a series of strategic spin-offs, these metrics have reignited interest in IBM shares. However, skeptics question whether these efforts can reverse years of stagnation in core segments.

The IBD Big Çap 20 Index is a curated list of large-cap performers, including IBM. Potential investors seeking stable picks often consult this index. To evaluate IBM's fundamentals, you can refer to the IBD Stock Checkup Tool and other specialized research platforms.

Broader market forces usually have the most significant influence on a share's price, overshadowing the unique potential of a single company. Technical elements, such as chart patterns and historical price trends, offer insight into short-term movements, while fundamentals like revenue and profitability drive longer-term potential.

Day-to-day stock prices depend on investor sentiment, market trends, and global events. Over a longer period, however, a company's shares are more likely to align with its actual performance, guided by earnings and strategic direction.

Large fluctuations in share prices can arise from macroeconomic indicators, changes in interest rates, or major political developments. While these events can cause volatility, informed investors also consider a company's fundamentals, including overall revenue, cash flow, and product pipeline.

During the exuberance of the late 1990s, many tech stocks soared despite weak profitability, eventually leading to the dotcom crash. Likewise, in today's markets, momentum can drive some stocks to inflated levels ahead of a correction.

For IBM, the lack of positive news since the last quarter continues to heavily influence investor confidence. Although the company's diversification strategy has merit, observers and analysts are still awaiting evidence of a sustained turnaround in critical metrics.

Its extensive product portfolio and the ongoing pursuit of returns keep IBM in the spotlight. Forecast revisions after each earnings cycle typically establish new short-term resistance and support levels. The question is whether IBM can surpass expectations and satisfy the market's appetite for growth.

Thursday's spinoff saw IBM shed one of its largest divisions, prompting analysts to question the feasibility of its mid-single-digit growth targets. Since 2010, IBM's revenue has steadily declined from around 100 billion dollars to about 73.6 billion dollars in 2020, leaving many uncertain about a full recovery.

Ultimately, movements in a stock's price hinge on supply and demand. The direction of the broader market, or "Mr. Market," can overshadow company-level accomplishments. To properly gauge IBM's next steps, investors may need to closely monitor both its technical indicators and fundamental metrics.

Chapter 13 - Fossil Fuel Sector and Correlations Studies

The Fossil Fuel Sector belongs to the Energy Sector; however, in this chapter, we will only cover the Fossil Fuel group of stocks, and we will temporarily leave the broader energy, coal, and other segments behind.

Petroleum products are fuels derived from hydrocarbons containing petroleum and natural gas. In order to achieve mass balance in the global oil supply and demand, supply includes not only crude oil but also NGLs (various kinds of heavy, oil-like hydrocarbons), natural gas, coal, and renewable biofuels used as oil-product equivalents. These are incorporated into our definition of demand. All OECD-producing countries provide the MOS with data on oil production, complemented by information from governments, oil companies, and consulting firms regarding individual fields.

Oil refineries (crude oil and natural gas) and processors deliver recyclable products to end users (customers). These organizations are active in the marketing and distribution of crude oil and/or natural gas products. The largest volume of products in the industry consists of heating oils, including fuel and gasoline.

Companies involved in the downstream process include oil refineries, distributors of petroleum products, petrochemical plants, natural gas distributors, and retailers. Downstream oil and gas producers are closer to end users and consumers. For this reason, "oil and gas companies supply customers with petroleum products" and "downstream oil and gas companies have a say in the industry."

Our downstream company manages various chemical and product activities as part of an integrated value chain that trades refined crude oil and other raw materials across a range of products reaching global markets for domestic and commercial transportation and use. We produce and sell lubricants, bitumen, sulfur, and petrochemicals.

It markets and transports oil and gas, managing the infrastructure necessary to deliver them to the market. Our integrated fuel system markets and trades natural gas, LNG, crude oil, power, and $CO2$ emissions, and sells LNG as fuel for heavy industrial vehicles and naval vessels. Enbridge operates the largest oil pipeline network on the continent, is a leading operator of natural gas pipelines, and owns a natural gas supply company.

The complete product range includes base and finished oils produced at the ISO 90001-certified asphalt refinery in Lloyds, Alberta. Base oil has a high flash point, low aromatic content (industry-approved), a high aniline point, and low BTX levels. ConocoPhillips extracts oil from a variety of sources and processes, including horizontal drilling and hydraulic fracturing for shale in the United States, oil sands mining in Canada, deepwater drilling, and other conventional extraction methods worldwide.

The company is based in Columbus, Ohio, and distributes commercial products through its refineries in Lima, Ohio, and Superior, Wisconsin, where it partners in a joint venture with BP at the Husky Refinery in Toledo, Ohio. Husky produces both online and direct refining feedstocks, including kerosene distillate (KD), atmospheric fuel oil, and HVGO (Heavy Vacuum Gas Oil), derived from its conventional heavy crude oil from its asphalt refineries. In addition, Husky markets natural gas fuels that are used for domestic heating, commercial heating, and the production of natural compounds found in many common household products and building materials.

The oil industry refers to oil-related activities that process and refine crude oil into petroleum products, as well as the distribution, marketing, and transportation of those products (see upstream). It is also referred to as the oil industry or the oil field, covering the global processes of exploration, production, refining, oil transportation by tanker or pipeline, and the marketing of petroleum products. The midstream sector involves the transportation, processing, and storage of petroleum-related liquids, including refined petroleum products, natural gas liquids (NGLs), ethane, and propane.

In the first stage of the refining process, crude oil components are separated by atmospheric-pressure heating and subsequent condensation. A process called cracking is then used to produce more low-molecular-weight hydrocarbons. Hydrocracking involves heating crude oil under high pressure (up to 5,000 kilopascals) in the presence of hydrogen and metallic catalysts such as platinum, nickel, and palladium.

These molecules form smaller alkanes used in fuels, including propane, butane, pentane, hexane, heptane, and octane, as well as components of liquefied gas. The smaller hydrocarbons are then processed into longer-chain carbon molecules at refineries. The heavier hydrocarbon is then broken down into lighter alkenes, such as ethane, propane, and butane (useful for the production of plastics), resulting in a product rich in aromatic hydrocarbons (suitable for absorption in petrol and diesel).

The middle distillates refer to hydrocarbon products in the medium boiling range of crude oil, such as kerosene, diesel fuel distillate, heating oil, and gas oil. The gasoline and gas fractions formed from low boiling products are more valuable than the higher boiling fractions of hydrocarbon fuels and liquefied petroleum gas (LPG). Meanwhile, hydrocarbon fractions such as naphtha, kerosene, aviation fuels, and heating oil are feedstocks for the petrochemical industry.

This means the way a refinery operates with respect to producing a given product depends not only on the nature of the crude oil feedstock but also on the configuration of the refineries, the range and types of processes used to produce the desired product, and the refinery's overall setup influenced by specific market requirements. The volume and percentage of oil extracted from a refinery may not always meet customer needs.

Oil companies operating outside OPEC are affecting oil prices because they are not providing sufficient capital for new oil projects. The lead time is too long to develop new oil and gas installations, and these companies are not increasing their supply in response to favorable market conditions. As a result, many producers have reduced operations and supply over the past twelve months, giving numerous oil and gas companies a tailwind.

Apergis and Miller (2009) examined how structural oil market shocks affect stock prices in eight developing countries. This study analyzes the dynamics and correlations between volatility and spillover effects of crude oil prices on traditional equity markets, represented by major indices of European oil-importing countries (UK, Germany, France, Italy, Switzerland, and the Netherlands) and oil-exporting countries (Norway, Russia, and Sri Lanka).

Given the emergence of structural changes in the oil financial markets over the past three decades, it is vital to examine the existence of a structural break in the relationship between the share prices of oil technology and transportation companies and the price of crude oil.

Researchers have studied the relationship between oil markets, a crucial energy source, economic activity, and the effect of oil prices on traditional equity returns. Park and Ratti (2008) show that oil prices in the United States and twelve European countries have a negative effect on equity returns, while equity markets in Norway react positively to an increase in oil prices. The relationship between oil prices and stock yields has attracted substantial interest because oil price shocks can have a significant impact on stocks. Price changes can affect input factors for production and influence manufacturing costs.

In the pursuit of a long-term relationship between stock prices and oil prices, increases in sectors like oil and gas in the United States, as well as automotive components that depend on oil, are stronger. Changes in oil prices also affect stock markets and corporate returns in oil-exporting countries.

They observe that fluctuations in oil prices for oil and gas companies negatively affect equity market returns during the pre-crisis period, both at the sectoral and macroeconomic levels. The co-integration of these effects confirms the existence of a long-term equilibrium relationship between the stock index, crude oil price, and short-term interest rates in the S&P 500. Our view on these results is that the effects of stock market aggregation are subdued for sectors with sensitivity to changes in oil prices.

It is worth noting that the unconditional correlation between SSIS and other indices is higher in this study than in the DJSI case, which excludes an unconditional correlation with Brent crude oil.

This study uses weekly data covering the period between January 2 and February 3, 2015, to evaluate the short- and long-term relationship between crude oil prices and the stocks of oil, technology, and transportation companies. Prices are listed in US dollars as monthly average spot prices for barrels of West Texas Intermediate crude oil. Oil companies' stock market performance is measured by the NYSE ARCA Oil Index, where oil represents the change in the overall share price component.

Preliminary data show that daily stock returns are excessively volatile, a frequent occurrence in financial time series data. By comparison, Sadorsky (1999) used unrestricted VAR and GARCH models on weekly US data to reveal a significant short-term relationship between unexpected oil price changes and returns on the macroeconomic S&P 500 stock index. We conclude from this analysis that the equity returns of oil and gas companies in Nigeria fluctuated in response to the oil price shock during the first (fifteenth) period and again in the sixteenth to twentieth periods, when their equity returns began to react to the shock.

The sharp rise in oil prices in the latter half of 2007 and the first half of 2008 has led many to argue that increased speculation played a role in commodity markets; however, there is no evidence of heightened activity in these markets. Determining the relationship between oil prices and other variables that change over time goes beyond casual observations and relies on econometric analyses that let researchers control for other economic factors and investigate the relationship between oil prices and key macroeconomic variables. Although researchers at the Federal Reserve Bank of Cleveland have not proven that oil prices have a limited effect on stock prices, they suggest that analysts cannot predict how stocks will react to changes in oil prices.

In an analysis of the impact of an oil price shock on Norway (an oil-exporting country) and its stock market, Bjornland (2009) argues that higher oil prices represent an immediate transfer of wealth from oil importers to exporting countries, with medium- and long-term consequences depending on how the governments of oil-producing countries use the additional revenues.

The first and most obvious is that other factors in the economy, such as wages, interest rates, industrial metals, plastics, and computer technology, can offset increases in energy costs. One sector that is influenced by the price of oil is transportation, which relies heavily on petroleum fuels. Another possibility is that companies will become more sophisticated in analyzing futures markets and can anticipate changes in input costs, and that businesses may be better able to adjust production processes to offset additional fuel expenses.

In a paper by James Hamilton in late 2014, a macroeconomist and oil markets expert at the University of California, San Diego, it was suggested to estimate an equation correlating changes in oil prices with changes in copper prices, changes in 10-year Treasury yields, and changes in the dollar based on oil prices, in order to predict how the equation would measure the effect of demand shifts on the oil market. It is useful to remember that both the demand for and supply of oil respond to short-term price changes, and that substantial price adjustments are required to rebalance when demand moves with supply.

Andrea Pescatori, an economist at the International Monetary Fund (IMF), found that all variables were moving simultaneously in the same direction, but the relationship was weak. His sample showed no correlation, with a 95% confidence level.

This indicates there is some long-term correlation between oil and stock prices. However, there is no long-term correlation, and oil and stocks are only moderately correlated over a short time frame.

While oil prices affect companies and equities in the energy sector, oil and equities do not correlate over long periods. There is a perception that an increase in oil stocks correlates with a decline in oil stocks, and vice versa. However, the correlation in the relationship between oil and stocks is zero.

These findings suggest that crude oil prices and short-term interest rates in the S&P 500 are long-term determinants of stock price levels for oil-related, technology, and transportation companies. In the pursuit of a long-term relationship between stock prices and oil prices, the increases are strongest in the oil, gas, and auto parts sectors in the United States, which depend on oil. By comparison, with a clear correlation between oil and equity prices, the state of oil and equities complements each other cyclically.

Share prices rise and fall based on future corporate earnings reports, intrinsic value, investor risk tolerance, and a host of other factors. Given the emergence of structural changes in the oil and financial markets over the past three decades, it was necessary to examine the existence of a structural break in the relationship between oil technology and transportation companies' share prices and crude oil prices. This study uses spot prices for West Texas Intermediate (WTI) crude to measure the impact of oil prices on the market performance of these companies.

The purpose of this paper is to examine the long-term effect of crude oil prices on the stock prices of U.S.-listed oil technology and transportation companies. This article broadens the understanding of the relationship between oil prices and equity markets in Europe by testing long-term linear and asymmetric links at both the overall and sector levels.

In capital markets driven by oil and equity price setting, it is important to maintain perspective and remain as current and objective as possible. Opinions, news, research findings, analyses, prices, and other information from third-party websites are provided as general market commentary and do not constitute investment advice. Therefore, I accept no liability for any loss or damage, including any loss of profits, arising from the use of or reliance on such information, without limitation.

Whether you invest in individual stocks, equity funds, or ETFs, you need to know how the price of oil affects your shares. Predicting the future of the oil market is complex, especially for large oil-consuming countries that do not have significant oil reserves. In the crude oil market, we use the daily forward price of WTI, which is the reference price for the global oil market and serves as the benchmark for the current global oil market.

One sector that is strongly influenced by the price of oil is transportation, which relies heavily on petroleum fuels. Higher oil prices lead to increased costs for unrelated products and services, whether that means higher taxi fares, more expensive airline tickets, the cost of an apple shipped to California, or new furniture delivered to China. Oil producers and refineries earn a small proportion of profits from their stocks, while other companies earn slightly more or slightly less.

Oil prices are likely to rise in 2019 partly because Saudi Arabia, on the supply side, has bolstered the market with significant production cuts, according to Francisco Blanch, head of global commodities and derivatives research at Bank of America Merrill Lynch. If oil prices stabilize or rise to levels that make it more profitable for companies to drill and the global economy begins to recover, do not expect stocks to do much more than follow the trend. On the other hand, if oil rises, supply-chain constraints may not be a boon to the economy.

Researchers from the Federal Reserve Bank of Cleveland have not shown in their study that oil prices have a limited impact on stock prices, but their findings suggest that analysts cannot predict how stocks will react to changes in oil prices. At this point, it appears that the global economy is on the verge of recovery, and oil consumption is rising, indicating we may be at the start of a bull market. The concern seems to be that oil will surge and prices will remain high for a long time.

Apergis and Miller (2009) examined how structural oil market shocks affected stock prices in eight developed countries. The results of an observational study conducted by Forbes showed a moderate correlation, with significant positive and negative correlations over the 1991–2011 period. Our view on these findings is that the effects of stock market aggregation are subdued due to the sensitivity of the sectors to changes in oil prices.

In this period of turbulent increases in oil prices and the stock market, the rise in oil prices also indicates higher production costs and inflationary pressures, which are synonymous with stronger-than-expected economic growth and increased consumer and investor confidence. Emanuel notes that stocks bottomed on December 26, while U.S. crude hit a low on December 24.

Determining the relationship between oil prices and other variables that change over time goes beyond occasional observations, relying on econometric analyses that allow researchers to account for other economic trends and examine the relationship between the price of oil and key macroeconomic variables. Recent research, however, suggests that there is only a small correlation between oil prices and stock prices over time. European Market Index (DJ Stoxx 600) and Crude Oil Price (Brent) 31. We believe that weekly data capture the interaction between oil and equity price changes better than daily or monthly data.

Share prices rise and fall based on future corporate earnings reports, intrinsic value, investor risk tolerance, and a host of other factors. It is common to correlate changes in an important price component, such as oil, with the performance of major stock market indices. One sector heavily influenced by the price of oil is transportation, which is particularly dependent on petroleum fuels.

While oil prices affect companies and stocks in the energy sector, oil shares do not correlate over an extended period. Oil stocks shift back and forth over time with a negative correlation. There is no long-term correlation, and oil stocks correlate significantly only over a short time frame.

By comparison, crude oil prices from 2008 to 2010 showed a positive correlation with equities, a negative correlation with the value of the U.S. dollar for most of 2007 to date, and an irregular negative correlation with bond prices between 2008 and 2010. Over the years, oil and stocks have risen and fallen together, so one might be tempted to conclude that they have a "positive" correlation, meaning they move in a similar direction. However, the correlation is zero, and they have no relationship at all.

As we have already noted, the positive correlations with stocks and oil arise because they respond to underlying shifts in global demand. Because bond prices and interest rates move in opposite directions (for example, the price of U.S. Treasury bonds), the price of crude oil tends to shift over time in the opposite direction due to changing economic conditions. As a result, crude oil and other commodity prices generally move in the same direction during periods when the likelihood of a worsening financial crisis diminishes or when the stock market recovers.

In most cases, the coefficient of one is positive, indicating a strong long-term relationship between sector share prices and the rise in oil prices. Our reasoning behind this result is that it is a stock market aggregation that is dampened by the sensitivity of sectors to changes in oil prices. For example, changes in the oil price are accompanied by similar changes in copper prices, and the breakdown proposed by James Hamilton, a macroeconomist and oil market expert at the University of California, San Diego, concludes that stocks and oil respond to common global demand factors.

In turn, the prices of corn, soybeans, and wheat are more volatile than total U.S. agricultural exports, indicating this volatility is shown in Figure 1, which charts price changes for these commodity exports and crude oil imports over time. The darker color in the chart indicates a high correlation and co-movement among the daily price movements of crude oil futures and several other commodity futures that are calculated for each quarter. The indicated prices are the monthly average spot prices for a barrel of West Texas Intermediate crude oil in U.S. dollars.

The historic drop occurred on April 20, when the price of West Texas Intermediate crude fell by more than 300% and traded at minus $37 a barrel. The price of oil recovered quickly, rising above $90 in May, marking its best month on record for West Texas. In this period of turbulent oil price increases and stock market gains, oil prices have also indicated higher production costs and inflationary pressures, which are synonymous with stronger expected economic growth and higher consumer and investor confidence.

The sharp rise in oil prices in the first half of 2007 and the latter half of 2008 has led many to argue that increased speculation in commodity markets played a role, indicating heightened activity in these markets. The results of this study show that there is a significant short-term link between oil price fluctuations and emerging markets. Although the researchers in the Federal Reserve Bank of Cleveland study have not shown that oil prices had a limited impact on stock prices, their research suggests that analysts cannot predict how stocks will react to changes in oil prices.

Crude oil is an important input for agricultural production, which means its price is a key factor tied to the costs of maize, soybeans, and wheat. Over time, growers use increasing amounts of energy to produce these crops. People fear that expensive fuel will hurt the economy, meaning higher oil prices will lead to lower stock prices. Lower oil prices mean we have more money to spend, and people assume that is good for stocks.

Between 2010 and 2016, the combined costs of chemicals, fuels, oil, lubricants, and energy in the United States amounted to 88% of the total costs for corn farmers, 98% for soybean farmers, and 104% for wheat farmers. As crude oil prices rise, the production of raw materials such as soybeans and wheat becomes more expensive, and farmers pass higher costs on to consumers. It is possible that companies will become more differentiated in how they analyze future markets and anticipate changes in costs, and that they will be better able to adjust manufacturing processes to offset higher fuel expenses. In the case of the U.S., households and businesses may sense that the Fed will not pay much attention to inflation and thus believe that economic shocks from rising oil prices will lead to higher inflation, adjusting their expectations accordingly.

One possible reason for the positive correlation between the benchmark S&P 500 stock market in 2008–2010 and crude oil, one of the world's most traded commodities, is economic expectations. This study uses the spot price of West Texas Intermediate (WTI) crude oil to measure the impact of oil prices on the stock market performance of oil technology and transportation companies. Given the emergence of structural changes in the oil and financial markets over the past three decades, it was important to examine the existence of a structural break in the relationship between these companies' share prices and crude oil prices.

Oil inventories offer insight into the balance between supply and demand in the oil market and, of course, can affect oil prices. For instance, changes in the oil price are often accompanied by similar changes in copper mining prices, as James Hamilton, a macroeconomist and oil market expert at the University of California, San Diego, has pointed out, concluding that oil stocks respond to common global demand factors. This study uses weekly data covering the period from February 2, 1990, to February 3, 2015, to evaluate the short- and long-term relationship between crude oil prices and the shares of oil technology and transportation companies.

Chang, McAleer, and Tansuchat use daily data on spot, future, and forward prices for WTI and Brent crude oil, as well as returns on the NYSE, FTSE100, and Dow Jones S&P 500 from January 2 to November 4, 2009. It takes time for product prices to level off and for markets to respond to changes in supply and demand, but in the case of oil, the price adjustment is immediate. As a result, stock prices for crude oil and other commodities generally move in the same direction during periods when the likelihood of a deepening financial crisis diminishes or when a recovery takes place.

By comparison, crude oil prices from 2008 to 2010 showed a positive correlation with equities, a negative correlation with the value of the U.S. dollar for most of 2007 to date, and irregular negative correlations with bond prices between 2008 and 2010. When oil inventories fall, investors take this as a sign that demand is rising and buy into the market, driving up prices. However, the observed correlation movements are influenced by changes in the price of crude oil and the values of other asset classes, which can be uncertain.

An estimated ten analysts and traders expected that U.S. oil inventories would drop by 2.5 million barrels from the previous week, with seven analysts predicting a decline and three forecasting an increase. The relationship between supply and demand is one of the core principles of economics, but it is not always clear when evaluating the impact of the ups and downs of crude oil inventories on commodity markets. Economic conditions can cause commodity prices, including oil, to rise or fall.

Oil prices rose by more than 4% on Wednesday, extending gains from the previous session as stronger risk appetite offered support while data showed an unexpected increase in U.S. oil inventories. Distillate inventories, which also include heating oil and diesel, were expected to have fallen by 2.3 million barrels in the previous week. Comparing the projected and actual declines in oil prices, we find that the 40–45% drop in oil prices since June 2014 is due to weak demand.

U.S. crude inventories are anticipated to have fallen slightly compared with the previous week, according to a Wall Street Journal survey of analysts and traders, based on data released Thursday by the U.S. Department of Energy.

Wednesday's gains came despite a rise in U.S. crude inventories for the first time since May. The increase in crude stocks was larger than expected and implies weaker demand that is manageable for crude oil prices.

The basic concept behind oil "ticket" prices is that of a company that holds inventories exceeding its obligations and offers to cover the organization's liabilities. Tickets provide an alternative to acquiring oil inventories to build or rent the required storage capacity.

John Petrides, Portfolio Manager at Tocqueville Asset Management, spoke about energy markets in an interview with CNBC's Trading Nation. He indicated that markets are at a critical point because they are in earnings season.

John Wiley & Sons, Inc. was founded in 1807 and has been, for more than 200 years, a valuable source of information and knowledge, helping people around the world meet their needs and fulfill their ambitions.

Global Welfare Implications for the World: OPEC reserve capacity for various oil-importing and oil-exporting regions is calculated based on local GDP gains and losses after changes in oil production.

One proposal is the reinstatement of the Energy Emergency Office to work with industry to gather better information about global oil inventories. Another improvement is a global data system that provides producing and consuming countries with an early warning system in the event that production and supply levels become unbalanced with demand and consumption. Section 2 offers a historical perspective on the functioning of the global oil market without OPEC in the years 1990–2018 by quantifying the role of spare capacity in the historical development of global oil production, oil price volatility, and the joint development of short-term supply and demand elasticity in the comprehensive context of an autoregressive structural vector (VAR) of the world oil market. Having established a counterfactual level of global oil production without OPEC's reserve capacity and the structural VAR model for the world market using a full sample, we can see how oil prices might have evolved had OPEC possessed a reserve capacity cushion and played a balancing role since February 1992.

Saudi Arabia and other OPEC members are trying to reduce production to support oil prices. In the 1980s, OPEC began setting production targets for its member countries, which were reduced as oil prices rose. On Sunday, the oil producers of the OPEC+ group agreed to initially reduce production by 9.7 mb/d above the previously agreed base price of one dollar.

Crude oil prices have risen over time as OPEC's production targets have been lowered. In particular, OPEC's largest crude producer, Saudi Arabia, often impacts oil prices. All major fluctuations in oil prices in recent history can be attributed to changes in the production levels of Saudi Arabia and other OPEC countries.

As of September 2018, thirteen countries accounted for an estimated 44% of global oil production and 81.5% of the world's proven reserves, giving the Organization of Petroleum Exporting Countries (OPEC) and Beijing substantial influence over global oil prices, which are determined by the so-called "Seven Sisters" of major oil companies. In 2016, in addition to the formal OPEC member states, ten other oil-exporting countries led by Russia joined the OPEC cartel to work together to set global crude prices by agreeing to production quotas that keep worldwide production aligned with demand and consumption. However, there is no conclusive evidence that non-OPEC countries are equally influential in determining the price of crude.

In response to dynamic economic and geopolitical trends, OPEC has adjusted its oil production capacity, which has affected the oil supply and led to volatility in oil prices. At various times, OPEC members have engaged in overtly anti-competitive cartel behavior outside the OPEC+ agreement on oil production and prices.

Moreover, stability offers an important advantage for OPEC members and other oil-producing countries in the developing world, where oil export revenues account for a large share of global export earnings (73% on average for OPEC+ since 2005).

When Saudi Arabia attempts to gain market share through discount pricing, American oil and gas producers, including the fracking industry, will feel the pain. Lower prices affect the livelihoods of millions of people in the oil industry and its extensive supply chain, and they can undermine the economies of weaker nations where social stability is already fragile.

In the long run, OPEC, which holds four-fifths of the world's proven crude reserves, is expected to depend on supply to maximize any additional barrel of demand. Tom Kloza, global head of energy analysis at Oil Price Information Service, stated that fuel prices could rise this year as demand drops due to hurricanes and refinery outages. However, other analysts say there is still considerable capacity that could limit price increases.

What we need from OPEC is recognition that we have worked with them to understand that market demand for crude will not increase in the second quarter as many of them have claimed in the United States, but at some point in other places.

OPEC is attempting to moderate oil prices, but its influence is limited by factors beyond its control. Oil inventories have fallen to levels that threaten global economic growth as OPEC and non-OPEC producers increase production. In the United States, for example, oil inventories were 6% below the five-year average in mid-June, according to the Energy Information Administration.

If OPEC exhausts its maximum production capacity, it will lose its ability to influence oil prices. The impact would be stronger if wars and civil unrest result in prolonged supply disruptions.

A decline could undermine the oil industry's ability to develop the technology needed for a clean energy transition worldwide.

In the final weeks before this book was written, many of my constituents contacted me to express serious concerns about the recent dramatic rise in oil prices. For example, uncertainty about the future level of oil demand is reflected in a broad range of potential major investments in OPEC member countries. We are encouraged by the unity shown by policymakers from producing and consuming countries who work together to meet this historic challenge and bring stability to the oil market.

The main challenges facing the 2021 program include further implementation and streamlining of more comprehensive regulatory measures such as the European Union's CO2 emissions regulations for cars and trucks, China's NV mandate, and California's Zero Emission Vehicle (ZEV) mandate. Other challenges include strengthening the electric vehicle ecosystem, charging infrastructure, and power systems, as well as integrating sustainable batteries to determine the long-term use of electric vehicles. Early indications from the new administration have prioritized fuel-economy standards, encouraged the development of charging stations, and provided tax credits to help factories convert combustion-engine vehicles to electric vehicles.

Federal funds intended to stimulate consumer demand and improve manufacturers' investment in building electric vehicle infrastructure should be conditional on essential job quality and domestic requirements. Existing support for electric vehicles, including the federal electric vehicle tax credit, lacks labor requirements, and several lawmakers have proposed linking job quality to future funding to boost domestic production of clean-vehicle technologies.

The rapid transition from dependence on internal combustion engines (ICEs) to battery-electric vehicles (EVs) is essential for reducing greenhouse gas emissions to avoid the catastrophic consequences of climate change, and it represents a major opportunity for the U.S. automotive industry. Many manufacturers are investing heavily in technology for electric vehicles.

Hybrid and plug-in electric vehicles will help improve fuel economy, reduce fuel costs, and lower emissions. As the energy transition and the broader transformation of the transportation sector into electric vehicles and regulated, fuel-efficient internal combustion engines (ICE) advances, global demand for refined oil products is expected to peak in the mid-2030s. In 2019, the United States imported about three percent of the petroleum it consumed domestically, and transportation accounted for 30% of total U.S. energy demand and 70% of U.S. petroleum consumption.

As we consider how transportation electrification fits into the broader energy transition, traditional oil companies should prepare for a global Corporate Sustainability Assessment (CSA) report not only for an expected peak in motor oil demand. These forecasts anticipate greater market shares for electric vehicles, stricter regulation of end-user emissions, and substantial material implications for two new issues that both CSA and automotive companies must address: (1) battery range and (2) battery lifecycle performance. These issues need to be tackled in order to advance the energy transition and address the average fuel consumption and emissions of battery-electric vehicles, which means reducing vehicle consumption and emissions and minimizing associated waste.

In order to reduce increasing CO2 emissions and air pollution in cities, it is important to provide more vehicles with electricity. The impact of charging infrastructure on new sales of electric vehicles is estimated at around nine percent, suggesting that early investment in charging infrastructure is a crucial first step in the transition to vehicle electrification. As momentum in electric vehicle sales continues in China, favorable access to transportation for new energy vehicles in certain cities must be reinstated.

According to the International Energy Agency (IEA), two to three million of the one billion vehicles globally are pure battery-electric or plug-in hybrid electric vehicles. The world's largest markets for electric vehicles are the United States and China, but electric vehicles also have a substantial market share in European countries such as the Netherlands and Norway. One major advantage of these vehicles is that they consume almost no fuel and produce no end-user emissions.

In Germany, for instance, the government reduced the value-added tax on low-emission vehicles from 19% to 16% and doubled existing subsidies for electric vehicles priced below $45,000 to $7,000. Private customers who purchase an electric vehicle that costs $50,000 receive an incentive of $8,000, while those who already have $7,000 and want to retire their old cars benefit from earlier value-added offers and scrappage programs designed to put more eco-friendly models on the road. Consumers are also offered generous clean-air incentives of up to $2,500 per vehicle, and California provides a $7,500 tax credit for electric vehicles. What is happening in the U.S. not only delays the rollout of electric vehicles to limit carbon dioxide emissions but also improves local air quality in cities by shifting emissions from vehicles to power plants.

The payback period, according to senior energy systems analyst Jarod Cory Kelly of Argonne, depends on factors such as the size of the electric vehicle battery, the fuel consumption of the gasoline engine, and the electricity generated to charge the electric vehicle. The initial costs can be offset by savings in fuel expenses, federal tax credits, and government incentives for utilities. The CAP recommends vehicle exchange and rebate programs to convert ICE vehicles and fleets to electric vehicles.

Developed by Argonne National Laboratory in Chicago, the model covers thousands of parameters, from the type of metals used in electric vehicle batteries to the amount of aluminum and plastic in cars. Jarod Cory Kelly, a senior energy systems analyst at Argonne, stated that electric vehicles produce more carbon than internal combustion engines and vehicles initially, due to the extraction and processing of minerals in battery production and electric cells. This model, along with other tools, is used by the U.S. Environmental

Protection Agency (EPA) and the California Air Resources Board (CARB), the two leading vehicle emissions regulators in the United States, to help shape policy.

Graff and Zivin concluded that plug-in electric vehicles, such as the Nissan Leaf, emit less carbon dioxide in certain regions than hybrid electric and gasoline cars and are less dependent on coal in Western U.S. states, particularly Texas. To determine the impact of electric vehicles on fuel demand, we must make assumptions about the total distance covered by electric vehicles relative to internal combustion engine (ICE) vehicles. To estimate this, we must also first make an assumption about the fuel consumption (energy and oil) of each vehicle and the amount of CO2 emissions involved in producing and using that fuel.

Chapter 14 - Raw Materials Sector and Correlation Studies

The raw materials enterprise includes a massive variety of groups that produce raw materials for different industries such as production, mining, chemicals, plastics, building materials, paper, forestry, packaging, metals, and other minerals. The materials sector consists of businesses involved in the discovery, development, and processing of raw materials like gold, oil, and timber. Companies in the materials sector are engaged in the physical procurement, development, and initial processing of products known as raw materials.

The raw materials sector includes organizations active in metals, refining, mining, oil, forestry, and chemical products. These raw materials are developed and sourced by other industrial sectors. The raw materials from companies in this sector are refined and sold for use in various industries and sectors.

The materials industry includes companies that manufacture and process chemicals, building materials (bricks, cement, containers, packaging), metals, glass, plastics, cardboard, forest products (wood, paper), metals and mining (aluminum, steel, copper, gold, and silver). The raw materials sector also includes companies in the mining, metal processing, chemical product, and forestry segments.

These include companies that extract and process aluminum ore (also referred to as bauxite) and companies that recycle aluminum to produce new products. For stock classification, the most common materials in this sector are mined products like metal ores, forest products, and timber. The raw materials sector is an industry that includes companies leading the process of discovering, developing, and processing raw materials such as timber, metal extracts like silver, gold, and aluminum, along with raw materials for energy production such as crude oil, coal, and gas. All of these are considered part of the materials sector.

Subsector Description: Raw materials chemical companies produce base chemical materials including plastics, synthetic fibers like viscose, nylon, and polyester, films, paints, pigments, explosives, and petrochemicals (chemicals derived from petroleum). Subsectors Description: Forestry products companies produce wood and other wood-based products, including lumber.

Companies in building materials produce primary construction supplies such as sand, clay, and gypsum, which are used in plaster, chalk, lime, cement, concrete, and bricks.

One organization offers electronics and construction materials, textiles, resins, adhesives, solar cells, and other products. Its Advanced Materials Segment provides copolyesters, cellulose esters, polyvinyl butyral (PVB) sheets, window protective films, aftermarket film products, value-added consumer materials, transportation consumables, durable construction materials, and products for health and well-being markets. The company was founded in 1961 and is based in Luxembourg City, Luxembourg.

Another company began with the industrial production of polymers from raw materials sourced from plastic waste at its site in Germany. On May 26, it joined other leading plastics companies, Dow and Nova Chemical, in founding the Closed Loop Circular Plastics Fund to invest in scalable recycling technology, system improvements, and infrastructure solutions.

A separate company operates in three segments: Americas Materials, Europe Materials, and Building Products. The commodities sector is among the three largest in the US because it is active in the oil segment. The apparel and hotel industries are overshadowed by large consumer-goods companies, which are sensitive to economic fluctuations, with Tesla representing over forty percent of its market capitalization.

As the economy grows, strong competition in the materials sector tends to limit the ability of companies to earn large profits, affecting share prices. Materials companies tend to perform well when the economy is booming, making them more attractive in a bull market. Good materials companies often have multiple business lines, investment-grade bonds, low debt, and low production costs, which help them remain profitable even if prices decline.

During economic slowdowns, demand for products and prices often decrease, lowering companies' share prices and profitability. For most commodities, including oil, timber, and metals used in construction and packaging, changes in the economic cycle can affect performance.

Cutlery makers, jewelry companies, and industrial fertilizer firms are not considered part of the raw materials sector because they work with raw materials in their fabricated form. Determining whether companies using these materials qualify for inclusion in the sector is important.

One of the world's leading mining companies, London-based Rio Tinto, concentrates on key industrial metals such as iron ore, aluminum, and copper, as they are widely consumed in the global economy.

A commodity company's success depends on demand for its resources, which in turn depends on demand for the final products in which these resources are used. Chemical and specialty chemical companies produce goods that people buy regardless of the economic climate. As a result, these companies often have strong pricing power and are less dependent on commodity prices, making them reliable dividend payers.

Although companies in the basic materials sector face risks tied to the broader economy, good materials companies are poised to benefit from diversified business portfolios. Commodities like Tredegar Corp. (TG), CRH Plc (CRH), LyondellBasell Industries (LYB), and Vedanta (VEDL) are examples of material stocks worth considering. Material stocks often do well in strong economies.

Copper and copper alloy products are used in construction (44%), transportation equipment (19%), electrical and electronic products (18%), consumer goods and general products (12%), and industrial machinery and equipment (7%). Old scrap is turned into refined metal alloys and accounts for 170,000 tons of copper equivalent (9% of apparent consumption). After the Bronze Age ended and the Iron Age began, copper remained in demand and retained its significance alongside iron.

Notable copper alloys include bronze and brass. Copper and zinc, copper, tin, and zinc alloys can be strong enough to produce weapons and cannons (often called cannon metals). Copper-nickel (also called cupronickel) is favored for low-denomination coins. These features make copper an excellent material for electrical and electronic products, which account for roughly three-quarters of global copper use. Copper is the second-most conductive metal, behind silver, which is more expensive.

Copper's ease of manufacturing and thermal properties make it common in refrigerators and air conditioners. Significant quantities of copper are also used in buildings, not only in wiring and cladding but also for its appealing color. Copper is used in pure metal form when high malleability is needed, and in alloys such as brass and bronze (about five percent of total usage) for extra strength.

Copper offers many advantages and is the third most widely used metal worldwide. It is employed as a conductor of heat and electricity, a construction material, and as a component of various metal alloys such as sterling silver (used in jewelry), copper-nickel (used in making ship fittings and coins), and constantan (used in strain gauges, thermocouples, and temperature measurement). Copper appears in car engines and many home appliances (for instance, washers and dryers) and is also present in numerous household goods through its alloys with other metals.

Copper serves many industries, from construction to electrical and electronic products, machinery, transportation, and consumer goods. It is also essential in electronics. Copper products show up in building construction, electrical grids, electronic devices, transportation equipment, and household appliances.

Much of the copper produced worldwide goes to the electrical industry. Remaining copper is alloyed with other metals to create various products. The major copper alloy categories, where copper is the primary metal, include brass (copper and zinc) and bronze (copper, tin, nickel, and silver). Many copper-nickel alloy combinations are fully miscible.

In practice, copper is most commonly used in electrical equipment (60%), in construction like roofs and plumbing (20%), in industrial machinery such as heat exchangers (15%), and in alloys (5%). Copper forms alloys with many metals and different alloying elements like zinc, tin, nickel, and aluminum. Many widely used alloys contain copper in combination with other metals.

In the UK, semi-finished products, also known as copper or pure copper and copper-alloy goods, often appear as wire rods, rods, plates, sheets, strips, foils, and tubes.

In electrical wiring, copper is used in heating elements, motors, renewable energy systems, internet cables, and electronics. It also appears in the decorative arts, where it is employed as an elementary metal in compounds and pigments. Copper has served as an architectural metal for centuries.

Copper is one of the few metallic elements that displays a natural color distinct from gray or silver. It is a vital element in silver carat gold solders used in the jewelry industry, altering the color, hardness, and melting point of these alloys. The copper-nickel alloy known as cupronickel is used in low-denomination coinage for the coin's outer cladding.

Copper produces numerous alloys, combining it with metals such as tin, nickel, and zinc to increase strength and other properties. This versatility makes copper indispensable in mechanical engineering. In addition to copper wiring behind walls and copper pipes in plumbing and other household electrical appliances, copper is also used in kitchens and bathrooms for its natural antimicrobial qualities. It is prized as a workable and attractive metal in artwork, including sheet copper sculptures, jewelry, signage, musical instruments, cookware, and more.

Though copper has countless applications, wiring in cables and products such as power lines, integrated circuits, transformers, and coils is the most familiar. Most people know copper for its use in home electrical wiring, but copper pipes are also used in plumbing for most residences and businesses.

Copper is ideal for these applications because it is the best non-precious metal conductor of electricity, making it both practical and economical. Copper and its alloys are regarded as durable and corrosion-resistant, which makes them useful not only for transporting drinking water but also in saltwater and other industrial environments.

Copper has become a preferred material in various industries, including electrical, construction, consumer electronics, and communications. Copper wires, pipes, and tubes are employed in building materials, plumbing, and the electrical sector. Copper wiring is standard in modern vehicles, and copper-brass has been used since the 1970s for radiators and oil coolers.

Electrical and consumer electronics products, like power cables, make up roughly one-third of all copper usage. Construction, including cables and water pipes, accounts for another sizable share.

There are many long-term factors that will continue driving global copper demand. According to a 2017 World Bank report on the increasing role of minerals and metals in a low-carbon future, the world could see demand for metals like copper grow tenfold by 2050 as we shift to renewable energy. If copper demand stays strong, fueled by global industrial expansion and robust prices, this change is likely.

Because of this wide usage, copper prices respond strongly to expectations about the global economy. In the short term, rising prices and emerging technologies might significantly impact demand for copper-based products.

Over the longer term, Chinese demand is expected to grow, potentially raising copper wire and cable prices for at least five years.

China drives the global copper market and represented more than two-fifths of worldwide demand in 2014. It is the world's largest copper consumer, purchasing nearly half of global output. Imports of raw copper products were up 98% from January to April compared to the previous year.

The London Metal Exchange copper benchmark set a record of 10,460 dollars per ton, topping 10,000 dollars. Emori noted that copper has become attractive to investors as major countries pursue decarbonization, which should boost demand for electric vehicles and wind and solar infrastructure. Besides electronics and home construction, copper also features in many manufacturing processes, so its demand can serve as an economic barometer.

Since 2011, copper demand has risen because of extraordinary growth in China, India, and other emerging markets. Copper prices rose about seven percent in the second quarter as economies worldwide began reopening. Global demand for refined copper plus recycled scrap is projected to increase by 4.2%, reaching 360 million tons at a value of 26.1 billion dollars in 2019.

This increase in copper demand stems from the strong construction of copper wiring and tubing, more investment in power lines and cables, and improved durable goods manufacturing. Currently, copper supplies are sufficient to meet anticipated demand based on usage projections in the next few years.

If demand continues to rise due to consumer and industry trends, copper's stable supply will persist. Even though the recycling rate is high and the industry can do more, recycling alone is not enough to meet future demand or ensure a reliable copper supply.

Although copper is widely recycled and the industry has potential for further improvements, recycling alone will not fulfill global requirements or guarantee a consistent copper supply. A sustainable mining environment, good environmental practices, and high recycling rates must all play a role in meeting copper demand. Circular-economy methods are critical for the long-term copper market.

Expect copper demand to grow with increased sustainable energy production and consumption, which fits governments' green energy ambitions. However, while copper stands to gain from this transition, the overall impact might remain moderate according to Smith. Long-term copper demand could be tempered if renewable energy expands extensively, because renewables can require more copper than traditional energy sources, according to analysts from Stifel.

Copper's supply and demand imbalances are not likely to resolve quickly. Price theory indicates heightened demand for scrap copper and substitution by other metals. Growth in electric vehicle production could drive up copper prices further through 2021.

Copper, like other commodities, is priced by supply and demand. When construction and electronics manufacturing grow, copper usage also increases. The metal's price is influenced by the global economy. When the economy is strong and consumers build houses and buy cars, copper is in demand and prices rise.

Refinitiv forecasts that Chinese copper demand growth will slow to about three percent, while moderate copper demand growth is expected in Europe, where construction and manufacturing are running above the global average. In the short term, the resurgence of industrial activity in China might cause supply-demand imbalances.

Copper supply and demand are considered to be in deficit as of April 2021, meaning demand exceeds available product. Canaccord Genuity Mining analysts predict Chinese stimulus will support copper demand, alongside a broader economic recovery anticipated in 2021.

Analysts suggest copper's surging price is likely to continue into 2021 due to tight inventories and robust demand, though at a more measured pace. Demand for copper has grown significantly in the last few years, pushing prices higher. Copper production, however, has often fallen short of expectations.

Copper is also seeing new demand from specialty metals used in electric vehicle batteries, such as lithium. The global mining sector has struggled to keep up, and investors view copper as a low-risk commodity. Increased consumption could drive copper prices higher, thus boosting shares in copper mining companies.

Copper is often considered a hedge against economic uncertainty, once overshadowed by gold and silver. Today, it is one of the most extensively used metals and plays a central role in both advanced and developing economies.

Copper sees strong industrial demand, which investors should note when building portfolios.

A combination of factors, including economic recovery, government policy, and rising inflation expectations, has driven metals prices upward. Copper's sharp rise has greatly contributed to the metals and mining sector's performance. With inflation moving higher, economic activity recovering, and the dollar weakening, copper encounters multiple supports. As a base metal, copper can also serve as an inflation hedge because costs are passed on at spot prices.

Recently, the copper industry felt pressure as the US prepared to raise interest rates, increasing the dollar's strength and reducing copper demand. China's announcement that it would release copper from national reserves to moderate prices was another blow to the industry.

Copper prices trended downward after 2011, reflecting declining global demand for industrial inputs due to weaker worldwide economic growth. Though copper currently trades at high levels, demand has not yet shown the consistency of past decades.

For now, copper prices hinge on US-China trade talks. Some believe that a potential agreement could support demand and prices. Bank of America projects copper could climb to 20,000 dollars per ton within three years. Analysts in the aerospace sector are concerned about copper supplies and potential bottlenecks in project pipelines, mining, and refining.

Because copper is a commodity, companies profit from the gap between production costs and the market price of copper. Fitch and other analysts believe copper will remain in short supply until around 2021. This could increase prices and motivate investment in new copper development projects to meet future growth. The housing sector depends on copper, so copper prices are strongly tied to construction activity.

The rate of mining and copper production determines the price paid by industrial consumers. Producers, suppliers, and users have to balance the costs of extraction, production, and distribution with overall demand. Global copper trading is highly efficient, often leading equity markets in emerging countries.

Companies and stocks most reliant on copper consumption and production can serve as vital copper price indicators. Additional references include commodity indexes for copper extraction and energy commodities like oil. The top copper stocks often show compelling value, earnings growth, or momentum, reflecting performance from mining and copper futures.

Producers cannot approve many significant mine developments until copper prices are sufficient, making them focus on expanding existing operations and limiting broader growth. Since copper prices affect profitability, investors often favor low-cost miners that can remain competitive when prices are down. The top three copper stocks typically have the best value, fastest earnings growth, or strong momentum, along with low price-to-earnings ratios.

When copper is traded in US dollars, a weaker dollar makes it cheaper in local currencies, thus increasing demand and affordability. For the metals mining industry, a weak dollar supports higher copper prices and vice versa. One significant risk in copper investing is the possibility of industrial users switching to alternative metals.

It is reasonable to presume copper's price correlates with global GDP. High-grade, low-cost miners with strong balance sheets and little debt can realize strong profits when copper prices rise, increasing their upside potential.

Contracts for Difference (CFDs) allow investors to speculate on copper prices without holding bullion, ETFs, futures, options, or mining stocks. However, investing in copper futures involves contango, which can erode value over time. Investors can avoid storage expenses by buying shares of companies operating in the copper sector.

This is not automatic, as mining and equity investors monitor metals markets for critical price points. A recent study examined the relationship between copper spot prices and overall stock market trends to see whether copper prices drive market fluctuations. A literature review in leading finance and business journals showed relevant research from the last three years on copper price fluctuations and the stock market.

The goal was to see if copper prices might foreshadow equity market volatility. Research suggested the S&P 500 could be set for a correction that establishes a price floor for copper. The market indices used included a copper index of copper-mining companies, a gold index of gold-mining companies, and a silver index of silver-mining enterprises.

Glencore is among the world's largest copper producers and distributors, giving it significant influence in the sector. Major copper development initiatives include large projects like the Olympic Dam Resolution Copper

Project in the US, targeting one of the biggest untapped deposits. Leading copper-producing countries strongly impact global production of the metal, supporting crucial industries worldwide and playing a central role in shifting to cleaner energy.

Chile is the largest copper producer globally, with 5.7 million tons of output in 2020. By 2018, Chile was producing 5.83 million tons, up from 5.5 million just a few years earlier. China is predicted to mine 1.7 million tons by 2020, making it the second-biggest copper producer.

Peru ranks as the second-biggest copper-mining producer in terms of capacity. Output has grown over the last decade, with China serving as a primary importer of Peruvian copper. Copper production in 2020 by country still shows Chile at the top.

In 2016, the ten leaders in copper production were Chile, Peru, China, the US, Australia, the Democratic Republic of Congo, Zambia, Canada, Russia, and Mexico. Global copper reserve data from 2017 indicated China had 27 million tons, making it sixth in copper reserves.

Morenci, located in Greenlee County, Arizona, is North America's largest copper producer. It is primarily owned by Freeport-McMoran (72%), with Sumitomo Corp. (15%) and Sumitomo Metal Mining (13%) of Japan owning the remainder. The Collahuasi copper mine, found 180 kilometers southeast of the Port of Iquique in northern Chile, produced 280,096 tons of copper in 2012, equivalent to 5.1% of Chile's total copper output. It is operated by Compañía Minera Doña Inés de Collahuasi, a joint venture among Anglo American (44%), Xstrata (44%), and a Japanese consortium led by Mitsui (12%).

The Buenavista Copper Mine in Sonora, Mexico, has operated since 1899 and is the oldest continuously active copper mine in North America, considered one of the largest porphyry-type deposits worldwide. Morenci in Arizona is North America's top copper producer. The El Teniente underground mine, 80 kilometers south of Santiago in the Andes, is the largest underground copper mine globally and is owned by state-controlled Codelco, producing 427,791 tons of copper and molybdenum in 2012.

Two Chilean mines produce copper, molybdenum, and silver, which Anglo American sells to offset costs. The Olympic Dam mine in Australia is privately held and contains some of the most significant copper, gold, and uranium deposits, as well as silver.

Copper mines in Saudi Arabia and Chile combined for 383 million pounds of copper in 2018. The lead-free copper mine in Zambia had 224 million pounds. Moreover, US-based companies account for the biggest share of South American copper production, with Chile and Peru together representing over 45% of global free-market production. In the US, Arizona, Utah, New Mexico, Nevada, and Montana are top copper-producing states.

Globally, copper is the third-most-used industrial metal, behind iron and aluminum. Key mining zones for copper ore include Africa, Australia, and South America.

Copper concentrates come from sulfur ores obtained via flotation and are then shipped for smelting. Mines also produce copper from oxide cathodes and sulfuric ores through leaching. Around 82% of known copper reserves come from sulfide ore mines.

Escondida remains Chile's biggest copper producer, reaching around one million tons annually. The Andina Division, located over 3,000 meters high in central Chile and comprising the Rio Blanco underground mine plus the Sur open-pit mine, produced more than 182,000 tons of copper in 2020. The Escondida copper mine in northern Chile's Atacama Desert is the largest copper mine in the world, producing 1.1 million metric tons during the fiscal year ending June 2013, or five percent of global copper output.

Russia's copper production rose from ninth to seventh globally, reaching 801,000 tons in 2020. The Mount Isa mine in Queensland, operated by a Glencore affiliate, treats 6.5 million tons of ore yearly. One of the biggest copper deposits is BHP's Olympic Dam copper, uranium, and gold mine in South Australia. Although best known for uranium, it is also one of the largest copper deposits globally.

The Chilean state copper corporation Codelco runs a major 3.4 billion dollar expansion that may extend one mine's life by 50 years. The Deziwa copper-cobalt mine and plant is part of a joint venture majority-owned by a Chinese metals mining company. In 2012, the Toquepala copper mine, 870 kilometers south of Lima in southern Peru, generated 152,000 tons of copper, 120,000 in concentrate and 32,000 in cathodes.

Rio Tinto also manages Oyu Tolgoi in Mongolia, one of the world's largest known copper and gold deposits, and the Kennecott Mine in the US, both expected to bolster output by 2023. Zambia, ranked eighth in global copper production, recently took complete ownership of the Mopani Copper Mine, where it previously held a 10% stake. Zambia has the world's largest cobalt reserves, and copper mining there is a top industry, producing about 1.3 million tons of copper in 2020.

Steven Gill, managing partner of the private equity firm Pala Investments, states that Chile, Peru, and the Democratic Republic of Congo will provide roughly 27% of the 15 million tons of copper mining projects projected to start up by 2030. This could spur higher prices, given volatile investment strategies. In Peru, which may outpace Chile in copper production growth, Chinese investment is expected to play a substantial role.

Copper pricing is linked heavily to each country's rate of growth. A key determinant of copper prices in emerging markets and the US housing market is whether the supply chain experiences disruption or substitution. Infrastructure needs in emerging markets are a major factor in copper pricing.

Natural disasters and wars can constrain mining and drive up copper prices. Political strife, environmental factors, and labor disputes also alter copper markets through effects on supply and demand. Nationalizing copper mines or strikes can disrupt production and raise prices.

Goldman Sachs, adopting a bullish outlook on commodities, suggests that Chinese copper demand is outpacing supply, but producers might struggle to meet it, which could lead to more price gains. If copper prices remain low, supply might contract as companies struggle to maintain production. However, changes in supply are not always immediately reflected in price movements.

Three-month copper on the London Metal Exchange hovers around 9,500 dollars per ton, remaining near 9,440.

The relative lack of enthusiasm indicates limited speculative involvement and fund positioning on the LME, CME, and Shanghai markets.

Copper prices are stable heading into the second quarter, and many anticipate a bull market for the red metal. Copper is receiving support from industrial usage. Other raw materials like iron ore and aluminum are also in demand.

Copper prices are influenced by the needs of emerging markets such as China and India, as well as by the US housing market's strength. Copper is traded on commodity futures exchanges, which creates volatility. Political instability in copper-producing areas, extended timelines for mining projects, and other industrial supply issues may also affect copper.

Those wanting to invest in copper should stay informed about developments in the copper market and may consult financial advisors. A recent copper mine strike underscores how labor actions can affect supply. Two Chilean copper mines experienced strikes, and a Canadian mine paused due to wildfires. Chile, which produces more copper than any other country, has had labor unrest that could strain the metal market. Labor conflicts can tighten supply at a time when demand for copper and other industrial metals is climbing.

Workers at BHP's Escondida and Spence copper mines in Chile sought to strike after arbitration with government and union officials failed. At Escondida, the world's largest copper mine, unionized workers turned down BHP's contract terms, choosing to strike. This is noteworthy because supply disruptions at a large mine can substantially impact copper prices.

The 1913–1914 Copper Country Strike in Michigan was a major event affecting copper mining in the region. Its mines stayed unionized for decades after.

In July 1913, numerous miners on the Keweenaw Peninsula began striking. A few days after that strike ended, the Ludlow Massacre occurred in Colorado, carried out by the National Guard in support of mining company interests, killing over a dozen unarmed women and children. This event prompted reforms in how miners were treated nationwide. The United Mine Workers of America led the Colorado Coalfield War beginning in September 1913, continuing much of that strike period.

Many miners labored in hazardous conditions for three dollars a day, and companies refused to raise wages. As copper prices declined and production increased, mining businesses sought to cut costs. New mines in resource-rich copper countries sometimes faced violent strikes led by the Western Federation of Miners to boost wages. Mining companies channeled their revenue from copper sales into profits rather than payroll.

Workers from established ethnic backgrounds, such as Cornish, Scottish, German, and Scandinavian, tended not to strike, whereas certain immigrant groups joined. Another reason miners struck was the paternalism system within the mining industry. Croatian workers, for instance, were paid less and assigned more dangerous tasks, so they joined the strike.

As a result, some mines introduced an eight-hour shift, allowing employees to spend more time at home. Copper miners wanted to stop using newer mining drills.

When labor unions go on strike while copper prices and global demand are high, it can be strategic, halting the flow of copper ore to the world market and causing price jumps. Strikes at large mines with significant numbers of unionized workers tend to lead to swift changes in copper prices.

Mining companies focus on labor expenses, but cyclical changes in ore quality and costs can be challenging.

Beyond copper, the wider materials sector includes building materials, chemical producers, paper, glass, packaging, forest products, minerals, and metal and mining companies. The raw materials sector includes businesses in metalworking, mining, oil, forestry, and chemical production. These raw materials are developed and sold to other industries.

The raw materials sector consists of companies that explore, extract, and process raw materials. It is an industry that develops the organizations leading the discovery and development of raw materials like timber, metals such as silver, gold, aluminum, and energy inputs including crude oil, coal, and gas as part of the materials industry. A commodity business delivers products and services from the earliest stages of extraction all the way to creating marketable end products.

By contrast, cutlery makers, jewelry producers, and industrial fertilizer firms are not in the raw materials sector if they only process raw materials in their basic form.

Material inputs are critical for modern society, and the sectors that produce raw materials serve other parts of the stock market. Stock in businesses that develop or acquire commodity goods is traded on exchanges, and some specialized funds invest in particular commodity groups.

Commodity and materials businesses can maintain profitability if they have investment-grade bonds, low leverage, and low production costs, even when prices are falling. These companies also often thrive when the economy is strong, making them appealing in bullish conditions.

Business cycles affect construction and land development. Companies making materials such as iron ore, steel, glass, and copper typically move in step with economic cycles. During economic expansions, intense competition may limit earnings, affecting stock prices. Stocks in copper, industrial gases, and specialty chemicals tend to excel during early economic recovery phases.

While basic materials companies do face economic risks, high-quality firms can draw on multiple business lines. Some exchange-traded funds (ETFs) track the MSCI World ex-USA Materials Index, which includes companies producing raw materials like BHP Billiton, BASF, and Rio Tinto.

A given fund might track the S&P 500 Materials Equal Weight Index, which is heavily weighted in chemicals, metals, mining, containers, and packaging. Another could track the StrataQuant Materials Index, which holds companies like Westlake Chemical, Alcoa, and Fastenal. Metals typically account for a large share of these funds, which also invest in chemicals, construction products, paper, and other industries.

Materials-focused ETFs might include shares of firms that extract, process, and develop raw materials such as metals, chemicals, and building products.

It is important to check whether companies that use these materials qualify for sector classification. Examples include companies that extract and process aluminum (bauxite) and those that recycle aluminum. Businesses that produce aluminum for construction and housing are also exempt.

Chemicals: These companies transform raw materials into industrial and synthetic chemicals like plastics. They produce, ship, and market chemical products used in agriculture, manufacturing, and electronics. Subsector Description: Building Materials companies make basic supplies like sand, clay, and gypsum used in plaster, chalk, lime, cement, concrete, and bricks.

Companies manufacturing do-it-yourself products, such as power tools, are excluded. Plastics companies are an overlap within the chemical industry, making plastic-based chemicals. Professionals in the chemical sector include chemical engineers, chemists, and lab technicians.

In 2018, the chemical industry made up 15% of US manufacturing. Chemical products span agricultural fertilizers, industrial gases, and specialty chemicals that are used in coatings and adhesives. Metals and mining cover various materials, such as gold, silver, steel, oil, and gold-based commodities.

The materials sector comprises producers in construction, metals and mining, and manufacturing. Because commodities including oil, lumber, and metals feed into construction and packaging, performance varies with economic cycles. As a result, construction, steel and mining firms, and manufacturers of finished goods all influence this sector.

Consumers encounter base chemicals, polymers, and specialty chemicals each day in household products: plastics, detergents, cosmetics, coatings, electronics, automotive finishes, and the materials that build homes. Some investors overlook companies that mine metals for electronics, produce seat fabric for airplanes, or create chemicals used in powerful medicines. The strategic advantages of investing in companies that deliver everyday essentials can make certain commodity stocks appealing to consumers.

Research by Windapo and Cattell found that transportation fees, crude oil costs, labor costs, and power costs are some of the factors influencing the price of building materials. Crude oil prices, energy costs, local taxes, fuel costs, electricity prices, high operating expenses, high raw material costs, shipping fees, and expensive labor raise building-material prices in Ghana's market. The study indicated a strong correlation among rising demand linked to global growth, dependence on imported construction materials, and cost increases.

When the economy expands, increased competition in the materials sector limits large profits, affecting share prices. Strong materials companies usually have multiple business lines, investment-grade bonds, low debt, and low production costs, so they can profit even when prices drop. They also perform better in growing economies, making them appealing in bull markets.

The materials industry is sensitive to changes in the global economy, the US dollar, and inflationary trends. Demand for commodities is cyclical, leaving industry participants exposed to shifts in economic performance. Materials-sector businesses are thus more vulnerable to economic conditions, although the best-performing firms often benefit from a diverse range of activities.

When the economy weakens, demand for commodities usually falls, bringing down prices. Commodity prices for metals and timber have dropped from their peaks. Some products have seen price increases but remain more stable and less volatile than many others.

Eventually, timber stocks should adjust for spikes in lumber prices. An earnings figure of 3.7 billion dollars is up 16% from a prior estimate that assumed lower lumber prices than the current forecast. Many analysts predict continued higher lumber prices.

Even if lumber prices decrease slightly, the levels seen recently are extraordinary, which could provide upside for timber stocks. Energy prices tend to lag in early inflationary cycles, as oil costs remain comparatively low at the outset.

Different market sectors alternate in delivering better returns as the economy moves through recovery, peak, and slowdown. When the economy moves into early recovery, industries sensitive to interest rates may outperform, and sectors experiencing strong demand during expansions often consolidate more robustly. On average, annual equity-market performance is above 1.4%, although inflationary pressure and energy costs can be muted in the early stages of recovery.

Equity sector returns shift across stages of the business cycle. Company earnings, interest rates, inflation, and other factors all move as the economy grows or contracts, influencing certain equity sectors more than others. This overview of eight stock-market sectors highlights those that typically show greater volatility over time.

Events such as war, revolution, famine, drought, strikes, political unrest, recessions, depressions, inflation, deflation, major industry bankruptcies, and shifts in supply and demand can drive share prices downward. The most volatile sector from December 31, 2009, to December 31, 2019, was energy, as it was hit hard by fluctuations in oil prices. According to S&P Global, this volatility was visible as the oil market swung rapidly.

Unlike stock investors, real estate investors can access certain tax benefits. For example, if you purchase an investment property, you can claim part of the purchase cost annually as depreciation. You cannot depreciate a stock purchase in the same way.

Oil producers and refineries earn part of their profits from equities, while some other companies earn slightly less. As oil prices increase, transportation becomes more expensive, and demand for substitutes rises. Companies respond

by innovating to reduce energy costs and increase profits, a hallmark of capitalist economies.

In periods of economic growth, there is heightened demand for industrial goods and services, boosting natural gas usage. Cyclic increases in consumption are prominent in industrial settings, which rely on natural gas as both a fuel and a feedstock for products like fertilizer and pharmaceuticals. If the cost of alternatives like coal or oil drops, demand for natural gas decreases and prices can decline.

A world map of major soil resources (Fe, Al, Cu, Zn) highlights differing distributions. Even though we have data on these resources in various locations, estimates of size, shape, and location are inconsistent. Initial global maps show that major metal reserves are scattered across developed and developing nations, with each metal following unique patterns.

Any correlation between GDP and in-use metal stocks varies by metal and over time. Researchers can estimate maps of unused metal stocks through linear relationships between global GDP and metal usage proxies. However, subnational data constraints limit the granularity of any analysis.

We note that intertrade intervals correlate strongly with NASDAQ equities data on daily timescales, regardless of trading volume. Each share has a crossover at the trading-day scale, where weaker or stronger correlations appear. This indicates no meaningful difference in correlation patterns for intertrade times between NASDAQ and NYSE stocks during the day.

Separate analysis suggests a positive link between correlation and price fluctuations over longer horizons for Nasdaq stocks, with a strong Pearson coefficient. Spread trading in LME metals is critical, but for aluminum it is especially dramatic because millions of tons stay off-exchange.

It is uncertain whether recent reforms will bring LME metal back to par with off-exchange storage. The rotation of warehouse metal may create confusion for the aluminum market. LME aluminum contracts seem to cycle through relatively tight conditions and high inventories, leaving the system with no clear resolution.

Holding inventory in anticipation of future use adds to LME's stock management challenges, alongside a reluctance to keep aluminum in official storage.

High exports of partially processed aluminum from China have pressured primary aluminum prices. Soft demand within China leads to surplus that is sold internationally.

Aluminum has experienced big swings in the last 15 years, especially during the commodity boom that followed the financial crisis. Prices fell sharply in 2009 during the global recession. Although aluminum prices then recovered from 2016 to 2018 due to production cuts, they have recently been lifted by strong demand and global stimulus.

Aluminum prices have climbed by more than 40% this year as demand has risen, aided by large stimulus packages, production cuts in China, and shipping disruptions. The aluminum market is tightening. According to the International Monetary Fund's long-term outlook, prices could reach around 2,276 dollars per ton by 2026.

US stock markets endured their steepest single-day decline since the 1987 crash, causing silver to plummet from 17.02 dollars an ounce to 12.01 dollars on March 19, a drop near 40%. After trading between 1,850 and 1,950 dollars per ton through late 2019, aluminum slipped to 1,700 dollars in early October 2019, reflecting weak Chinese demand, oversupply fears, elevated Chinese exports, and weaker local consumption.

Gold prices rebounded during a bear market rally in US stocks, surging on COMEX to an intraday high of 1,726 dollars an ounce on April 7.

Aluminum prices spiked to their highest in over a decade following the coup in Guinea, a key bauxite supplier. Financial and industrial metals such as silver were also hit by market volatility. Gold had been performing well, reaching a seven-year high of 1,684 dollars on March 6. Once it became clear on March 12 that the US economy would suffer severely, gold dropped with equities.

From mid-March onward, gold fell in tandem with the stock market, although it has since recovered as investors sense a renewed upturn.

- END -

About the Author

The low-profile, mysterious yet legendary investor Warren H. Lau has finally released his investing book series, "Winning Strategies of Professional Investment."

Warren H. Lau has spent more than ten years in the investment field.

He bet heavily on a rebound in the Chinese stock market during the 2008 subprime crisis and grew his portfolio by 600% within three years. Between 2010 and 2017, he increased his portfolio by 320% over seven years, achieving an average annual return of 22%. He successfully navigated the European debt crisis and the 2015 Chinese Black Monday and Tuesday. He credits these results to a combined application of fundamental, technical, and news analysis.

Warren H. Lau summarized his knowledge and experience in his investment book series, "Winning Strategies of Professional Investment."

Read more at https://www.inpressinternational.com/warren-h-lau.

About the Publisher

INPress International is a global publication organization that focuses on knowledges and topics where the traditional schooling system do not provide. Our Mission is to build a more humanistic, fair and peaceful future through our publication works. Check out our Website:

https://inpressinternational.com
Read more at https://www.inpressinternational.com.

About the Author

Meet Warren H. Lau – A tech CEO with a Wall Street assassin's past. Before revolutionizing the tech industry, he spent 10+ years crushing financial markets with a 600% return during the 2008 crash and 22% annual gains for 7 straight years (through Europe's debt crisis and China's Black Monday). His edge? A trifecta of fundamental, technical, and news analysis – a system so potent, hedge funds tried (and failed) to replicate it.

Fact: 97% of traders lose money guessing market moves.

Warren didn't just beat the odds – he rewrote them.

In 2008, Warren watched peers get wiped out. Instead of panicking, he saw blood in the streets = opportunity. His "back-against-the-wall" moment birthed a ruthless, rules-based system – now distilled into his Winning Strategies series.

Every trader knows the sinking feeling of waking up to a crashing portfolio - watching helplessly as losing positions drain your account while fees pile up. It's the frustration of clinging to hopeless stocks, praying for a rebound that never comes. But imagine the thrill of spotting a breakout before anyone else, executing your trade with precision timing, then sitting back as the market chases your entry point. That's the trader's high that comes from having a real edge in the markets.

These strategies weren't born in a Ivy League lab – they were forged in market hellfires, tested against:

• The 2008 Subprime massacre

• The 2010 European debt contagion

• China's 2015 "Black Monday" (where most traders got atomized)

Testimonials

◈ *"I went from $10k to $27k in 4 months using Warren's 'Crash-Proof' rules."*

– Jason R. (Performance Backed by MyFxBook Verification)

◈ "Finally, a trading book that doesn't read like a NASA manual."

– Lisa T. (Former teacher turned full-time trader)

Read more at https://www.inpressinternational.com/warren-h-lau.

iNPress
INternational

About the Publisher

INPress International is a global publication organization that focuses on knowledges and topics where the traditional schooling system do not provide. Our Mission is to build a more humanistic, fair and peaceful future through our publication works.

Check out our Website:

https://inpressinternational.com

Read more at https://www.inpressinternational.com.

www.ingramcontent.com/pod-product-compliance
Lightning Source LLC
LaVergne TN
LVHW090414210926
848480LV00002B/563
9798215543320